Hugo's Simplified System

German
Phrase Book

Hugo's Language Books Limited

This revised edition
© 1993 Hugo's Language Books Ltd/Lexus Ltd
All rights reserved
ISBN 0 85285 198 7

2nd impression 1995

Compiled by
Lexus Ltd
with
Chris Stephenson
and
Horst Kopleck

*Facts and figures given in this book were
correct when printed. If you discover any
changes, please write to us.*

Set in 9/9 Plantin and Plantin Light by
Lexus Ltd with Dittoprint Ltd, Glasgow
Printed in Great Britain by
Page Bros, Norwich

CONTENTS

Preface	4
Introduction, Pronunciation	5
Useful Everyday Phrases	6
Colloquialisms	17
Days, Months, Seasons	18
Numbers	19
Time	20
Hotels	23
Camping and Caravanning	29
Villas and Apartments	32
Motoring	37
Travelling Around	45
Restaurants	59
Menu Guide	64
Shops and Services	80
Sport	91
Post Offices and Banks	97
Telephones	102
Emergencies	108
Health	113
Conversion Tables	120
Mini-Dictionary	121

PREFACE

This revised and enlarged edition is the latest in a long line of Hugo phrase books and is of excellent pedigree, having been compiled by experts to meet the general needs of tourists and business travellers. Arranged under the usual headings of 'Hotels', 'Motoring' and so forth, the ample selection of useful words and phrases is supported by a 2,000 line mini-dictionary. By cross-reference to this, scores of additional phrases may be formed. There is also an extensive menu guide listing approximately 600 dishes or methods of cooking and presentation.

Highlighted sections illustrate some of the replies you may be given and the signs or instructions you may see or hear. The pronunciation of words and phrases in the main text is imitated in English sound syllables, and particular characteristics of German are illustrated in the Introduction. You should have no difficulty managing the language, especially if you use our audio-cassette of selected extracts from the book. Ask your bookseller for the Hugo German Travel Pack.

INTRODUCTION

PRONUNCIATION

When reading the imitated pronunciation, stress that part which is underlined. Pronounce each syllable as if it formed part of an English word, and you will be understood sufficiently well. Remember the points below, and your pronunciation will be even closer to the correct German. Use our audio-cassette of selected extracts from this book, and you should be word-perfect!

g   is pronounced hard as in 'get'.

KH   represents the guttural German 'ch' and should sound like the Scottish 'loch' (which isn't 'lock').

OO   represents the long German 'u'; make this an English 'oo' as in 'food' (not short as in 'foot').

oo   represents the shorter German 'u', as in English 'took', 'book'.

(n   is how we imitate the German 'ü', which sounds like the 'ee' in 'seen' if you pronounce it with rounded lips (or like the French 'u').

ow   should sound like the 'ow' in 'cow' (not as in 'low').

'YOU' AND 'I'

In most cases we have given the polite form for 'you' – which is **Sie** *zee*. The familiar form **du** *dOO* can also be used, but normally only if you are talking to someone you know well and would regard as a personal friend.

Questions involving 'I' have sometimes been translated with 'man', for example **Can I ...?** Kann man ...? Literally 'man' means 'one' but is not a formal word as it is in English.

5

USEFUL EVERYDAY PHRASES

YES, NO, OK ETC

Yes/No
Ja/Nein
ya/nine

Good/Excellent!
Gut/Ausgezeichnet!
gOOt/owss-guh-tsysh-net

Don't!
Nicht!
nisht

OK
Okay
okay

That's fine
In Ordnung
in ortnoong

That's right
Stimmt
shtimmt

GREETINGS, INTRODUCTIONS

How do you do, pleased to meet you
Guten Tag, freut mich
gOOten tahk froyt mish

Good morning/good afternoon/good evening
Guten Morgen/Guten Tag/Guten Abend
gOOten morgen/gOOten tahk/gOOten ahbent

Good night *(going to bed)*
Gute Nacht
gOOtuh naKHt

(leaving late at night)
Auf Wiedersehen
owf veeder-zayn

Goodbye
Auf Wiedersehen
owf veeder-zayn

How are you?
Wie geht es Ihnen?
vee gayt ess eenen

(familiar form)
Wie geht es dir?
vee gayt ess deer

My name's ...
Ich heiße ...
ish hice-uh

What's your name?
Wie heißen Sie?
vee hice-en zee

(familiar form)
Wie heißt du?
vee hice-t dOO

What's his/her name?
Wie heißt er/sie?
vee hice-t air/zee

May I introduce ...?
Darf ich Ihnen ... vorstellen?
darf ish eenen ... for-shtellen

This is ...
Dies ist ...
deess ist

Hello/Hi
Hallo
hallo

Bye!/Cheerio!
Tschüs!
chœss

7

See you later
Bis später
biss shpayter

It's been nice meeting you
Es war nett, Sie kennenzulernen
ess var nett zee kennen-tsoo-lairnen

PLEASE, THANK YOU, APOLOGIES

Thank you
Danke
dankuh

No thank you
Nein, danke
nine dankuh

Please
Bitte
bittuh

Excuse me!
Entschuldigung!
ent-shooldigoong

Sorry!
Entschuldigung!
ent-shooldigoong

I'm really sorry
Tut mir wirklich leid
tOOt meer veerklish lite

It was my fault/it wasn't my fault
Es war meine Schuld/es war nicht meine Schuld
ess var mine-uh shoolt/ess var nisht mine-uh shoolt

WHERE, HOW, ASKING

Excuse me please
Entschuldigen Sie bitte
ent-shooldigen zee bittuh

Can you tell me ...?
Können Sie mir sagen ...?
kurnen zee meer zahgen

Can I have ...?
Kann ich ... haben?
kan ish ... hahben

Would you like a ...?
Möchten Sie einen/eine/ein ...?
murshten zee ine-en/ine-uh/ine

Would you like to ...?
Möchten Sie ...?
murshten zee

Is there ... here?
Gibt es hier ...?
geept ess heer

What's that?
Was ist das?
vass ist dass

Where can I get ...?
Wo bekomme ich ...?
vo bukommuh ish

How much is it?
Was kostet das?
vass kostet dass

9

Where is the ...?
Wo ist der/die/das ...?
vo ist dair/dee/dass

ABOUT ONESELF

I'm from ...
Ich bin aus ...
ish bin owss

I'm ... years old
Ich bin ... Jahre alt
ish bin ... yaruh allt

I'm a ...
Ich bin ...
ish bin

I'm married/single/divorced
Ich bin verheiratet/ledig/geschieden
ish bin fairhyrahtet/laydish/gusheeden

I have ... sisters/brothers/children
Ich habe ... Schwestern/Brüder/Kinder
ish hahbuh ... shvestern/brooder/kinder

LIKES, DISLIKES, SOCIALIZING

I like/love ...
Ich mag/liebe ...
ish mahk/leebuh

I like swimming/travelling
Ich schwimme/reise gern
ish shvimmuh/ryzuh gairn

I don't like ...
Ich mag ... nicht
ish mahk ... nisht

I don't like swimming/travelling
Ich schwimme/reise nicht gern
ish shvimmuh/ryzuh nisht gairn

I hate ...
Ich hasse ...
ish hassuh

Do you like ...?
Mögen Sie ...?
murgen zee

It's delicious/awful!
Es ist köstlich/furchtbar!
ess ist kurstlish/foorshtbar

I don't drink/smoke
Ich trinke/rauche nicht
ish trinkuh/rowKHuh nisht

Do you mind if I smoke?
Haben Sie etwas dagegen, wenn ich rauche?
hahben zee etvass dagaygen ven ish rowKHuh

I don't eat meat or fish
Ich esse kein Fleisch und keinen Fisch
ish essuh kine flysh oont kine-en fish

What would you like (to drink)?
Was möchten Sie (trinken)?
vass murshten zee (trinken)

I would like a ...
Ich möchte gern einen/eine/ein ...
ish murshtuh gairn ine-en/ine-uh/ine

11

Nothing for me thanks
Nichts für mich, danke
nishts fwr mish dankuh

I'll get this one
Das geht auf meine Rechnung
dass gayt owf mine-uh reshnoong

Cheers!
Prost!
prohst

I would like to ...
Ich möchte gern ...
ish murshtuh gairn

Let's go to Stuttgart/go to the cinema
Wollen wir nach Stuttgart fahren/ins Kino gehen?
vollen veer nahKH shtootgart faren/inss keeno gay-en

Let's go swimming/for a walk
Wollen wir schwimmen/spazieren gehen?
vollen veer shvimmen/shpatseeren gay-en

What's the weather like?
Wie ist das Wetter?
vee ist dass vetter

The weather's awful
Das Wetter ist furchtbar
dass vetter ist foorshtbar

It's pouring down
Es gießt
ess geest

It's really hot/sunny
Es ist wirklich heiß/sonnig
ess ist veerklish hice/zonnish

HELP, PROBLEMS (see also *EMERGENCIES* p108)

Can you help me?
Können Sie mir helfen?
kurnen zee meer helfen

I don't understand
Ich verstehe nicht
ish fairshtayuh nisht

Do you speak English/French?
Sprechen Sie Englisch/Französisch?
shpreshen zee eng-lish/frantsur-zish

Does anyone here speak English?
Spricht hier jemand Englisch?
shprisht heer yaymant eng-lish

I can't speak German
Ich spreche kein Deutsch
ish shpreshuh kine doytsh

I don't know
Ich weiß nicht
ish vice nisht

What's wrong?
Stimmt etwas nicht?
shtimmt etvass nisht

Please speak more slowly
Sprechen Sie bitte etwas langsamer
shpreshen zee bittuh etvass langzahmer

Please write it down for me
Könnten Sie es mir bitte aufschreiben?
kurnten zee ess meer bittuh owf-shryben

I've lost my way
Ich habe mich verlaufen
ish hahbuh mish fairlowfen

(driving)
Ich habe mich verfahren
ish hahbuh mish fairfaren

Go away!
Verschwinden Sie!
fairshvinden zee

TALKING TO RECEPTIONISTS ETC

I have an appointment with ...
Ich habe eine Verabredung mit ...
ish hahbuh ine-uh fairap-raydoong mit

I'd like to see ...
Ich möchte gern ... sprechen
ish murshtuh gairn ... shpreshen

Here's my card
Hier ist meine Karte
heer ist mine-uh kartuh

My company is ...
Meine Firma ist ...
mine-uh feerma ist

May I use your phone?
Kann ich Ihr Telefon benutzen?
kan ish eer telefohn bunootsen

THINGS YOU'LL HEAR

Achtung!	attention, look out!
auf Wiedersehen	goodbye
bedienen Sie sich	help yourself
bis später	see you later

→

bitte	please
bitte?	pardon?
bitte (schön/sehr)	here you are, you're welcome
bitte (schön/sehr)?	what will it be?, can I help you?
danke	thanks
danke gleichfalls	the same to you
Entschuldigung	excuse me
genau	exactly
gut	good
guten Tag, freut mich	how do you do, nice to meet you
gute Reise	have a good trip
ich verstehe nicht	I don't understand
ich weiß nicht	I don't know
schöne Grüße an ...	give my regards to ...
stimmt	that's right
tschüs	cheerio
tut mir wirklich leid!	I'm so sorry!
Verzeihung	excuse me
vielen Dank	thank you very much
wie bitte?	what did you say?
wie geht es Ihnen?	how are you?
wie geht's?	how are things?
wirklich?	is that so?, really?

THINGS YOU'LL SEE

Abfall	litter
Aufzug	lift
außer	except
außer Betrieb	out of order
Ausgang	way out, exit

→

15

Auskunft	information
belegt	no vacancies
besetzt	engaged
Besuchszeiten	visiting hours
bitte nicht ...	please do not ...
Damen	ladies
drücken	push
Eingang	way in, entrance
Eintritt	entry
Eintritt frei	admission free
Erdgeschoß	ground floor
Feiertag	public holiday
frisch gestrichen	wet paint
Fußgänger	pedestrians
Gefahr	danger
geöffnet	open
geschlossen	closed
Herren	gentlemen
kein(e) ...	no ...
kein Zutritt	no admittance
nicht ...	do not ...
Nichtraucher	no smoking
Notausgang	emergency exit
nur ...	only ...
Öffnungszeiten	opening times
Raucher	smokers
Straße	street
Stock	floor, storey
Tiefgeschoß	basement
untersagt	prohibited
verboten	forbidden
Vorsicht	take care
ziehen	pull
Zoll	customs
zu verkaufen	for sale
zu vermieten	for rent, for hire

COLLOQUIALISMS

You may hear these: to use some of them yourself could be risky!

alles klar!	fine, great
Arschloch	bastard
bekloppt	crazy
bescheuert	crazy, daft
besoffen	pissed, smashed
Blödsinn	nonsense, rubbish
doof	stupid
du lieber Gott!	good God!
du spinnst wohl!	you've got to be joking!, you're out of your mind!
Kumpel	pal
Mann!	boy!
Mensch!	wow!
Mist!	shit!
nee	nope
Ossi	East German
sauer	pissed off
Scheiße!	shit!
Schnauze!	shut your mouth!
Schwachkopf	idiot, wally
Schwachsinn	rubbish
schwul	gay
Sonntagsfahrer!	Sunday driver!
Spitze	fantastic, magic
stark	great
super	great
toll!	tremendous!, brilliant!
Typ	guy, bloke
Unverschämtheit	cheek, nerve
verdammt noch mal!	bloody hell!
Wahnsinn!	fantastic!
Wessi	West German

17

DAYS, MONTHS, SEASONS

Sunday	Sonntag	*zontahk*
Monday	Montag	*mohntahk*
Tuesday	Dienstag	*deenstahk*
Wednesday	Mittwoch	*mitvoKH*
Thursday	Donnerstag	*donnerstahk*
Friday	Freitag	*frytahk*
Saturday	Samstag,	*zamstahk,*
	Sonnabend	*zonnahbent*
January	Januar	*yanOOar*
February	Februar	*faybrOOar*
March	März	*mairts*
April	April	*april*
May	Mai	*my*
June	Juni	*yOOnee*
July	Juli	*yOOlee*
August	August	*owgoost*
September	September	*zeptember*
October	Oktober	*oktober*
November	November	*november*
December	Dezember	*daytsember*
Spring	Frühling	*früling*
Summer	Sommer	*zommer*
Autumn	Herbst	*hairpst*
Winter	Winter	*vinter*
Christmas	Weihnachten	*vynaKHten*
Christmas Eve	Heiligabend	*hylish-ahbent*
New Year	Neujahr	*noy-yar*
New Year's Eve	Silvester	*zilvester*
Easter	Ostern	*ohstern*
Good Friday	Karfreitag	*karfrytahk*
Whitsun	Pfingsten	*pfingsten*

NUMBERS

0 null *nool*
1 eins *ine-ss*
2 zwei *tsvy*
3 drei *dry*
4 vier *feer*
5 fünf *fünf*
6 sechs *zex*
7 sieben *zeeben*
8 acht *aKHt*
9 neun *noyn*

10 zehn *tsayn*
11 elf *elf*
12 zwölf *tsvurlf*
13 dreizehn *dry-tsayn*
14 vierzehn *veer-tsayn*
15 fünfzehn *fünf-tsayn*
16 sechzehn *zesh-tsayn*
17 siebzehn *zeep-tsayn*
18 achtzehn *aKHt-tsayn*
19 neunzehn *noyn-tsayn*

20 zwanzig *tsvantsish*
21 einundzwanzig *ine-oont-tsvantsish*
22 zweiundzwanzig *tsvy-oont-tsvantsish*
30 dreißig *drysish*
40 vierzig *feertsish*
50 fünfzig *fünftsish*
60 sechzig *zeshtsish*
70 siebzig *zeeptsish*
80 achtzig *aKHtsish*
90 neunzig *noyntsish*
100 hundert *hoondert*
110 hundertzehn *hoondert-tsayn*
200 zweihundert *tsvy-hoondert*
1,000 tausend *towzent*
10,000 zehntausend *tsayn-towzent*
100,000 hunderttausend *hoondert-towzent*
1,000,000 eine Million *ine-uh mill-yohn*

Ordinal numbers are formed by adding **-te** or **-ste** if the number ends in **-ig**. For example, **fünfte** *fünftuh* 'fifth', **zwanzigste** *tsvantsishstuh* 'twentieth'. Exceptions are: **erste** *airstuh* 'first', **dritte** *drittuh* 'third' and **siebte** *zeeptuh* 'seventh'.

TIME

today	heute	*hoytuh*
yesterday	gestern	*gestern*
tomorrow	morgen	*morgen*
the day before yesterday	vorgestern	*forgestern*
the day after tomorrow	übermorgen	*@bermorgen*
this week	diese Woche	*deezuh voKHuh*
last week	letzte Woche	*letstuh voKHuh*
next week	nächste Woche	*naykstuh voKHuh*
this morning	heute morgen	*hoytuh morgen*
this afternoon	heute nachmittag	*hoytuh nahKHmittahk*
this evening	heute abend	*hoytuh ahbent*
tonight	heute abend	*hoytuh ahbent*
yesterday afternoon	gestern nachmittag	*gestern nahKHmittahk*
last night		
(last evening)	gestern Abend	*gestern ahbent*
(late at night)	gestern Nacht	*gestern naKHt*
tomorrow morning	morgen früh	*morgen fr@*
tomorrow night	morgen abend	*morgen ahbent*
in three days	in drei Tagen	*in dry tahgen*
three days ago	vor drei Tagen	*for dry tahgen*
late	spät	*shpayt*
early	früh	*fr@*
soon	bald	*balt*
later on	später	*shpayter*
at the moment	im Moment	*im moment*
second	die Sekunde	*zekoonduh*
minute	die Minute	*minOOtuh*
one minute	eine Minute	*ine-uh minOOtuh*
two minutes	zwei Minuten	*tsvy minOOten*

quarter of an hour	eine Viertelstunde	*feertelshtoonduh*
half an hour	eine halbe Stunde	*halbuh shtoonduh*
three quarters of an hour	eine Dreiviertel-stunde	*dryfeertel-shtoonduh*
hour	die Stunde	*shtoonduh*
day	der Tag	*tahk*
every day	jeden Tag	*yayden tahk*
all day	den ganzen Tag	*dayn gantsen tahk*
the next day	am nächsten Tag	*am nayksten tahk*
week	die Woche	*voKHuh*
fortnight	zwei Wochen	*tsvy voKHen*
month	der Monat	*mohnaht*
year	das Jahr	*yar*

TELLING THE TIME

To say the hour in German use the word **Uhr** *OOr* preceded by the appropriate number, for example: **neun Uhr** *noyn OOr* is 'nine o'clock'. The 24-hour clock is used much more commonly in Germany.

The word for 'past' is **nach** *nahKH*. So **zehn nach neun** *tsayn nahKH noyn* is 'ten past nine'. The word for 'to' is **vor** *for*. So **zehn vor neun** *tsayn for noyn* is 'ten to nine'. The word for '(a) quarter' is **viertel** *feertel*. So **viertel nach/vor neun** *feertel nahKH for noyn* is '(a) quarter past/to nine'.

The important thing to remember when telling the time is that when talking about the half hour, Germans count back from the next full hour, so that, for example, 'half past nine' is said in German as 'half ten'. So **es ist halb zehn** *ess ist halp tsayn* means 'it's half past nine'. Think 'half to' instead of 'half past'.

TIME

what time is it?	wie spät ist es?	*vee shpayt ist ess*
am	morgens	*morgens*
pm	nachmittags	*nahKHmittahks*
(in the evening)	abends	*ahbents*
one o'clock	ein Uhr	*ine OOr*
ten past one	zehn nach eins	*tsayn nahKH ine-ss*
quarter past one	viertel nach eins	*feertel nahKH ine-ss*
half past one	halb zwei	*halp tsvy*
twenty to two	zwanzig vor zwei	*tsvantsish for tsvy*
quarter to two	viertel vor zwei	*feertel for tsvy*
13.00	dreizehn Uhr	*dry-tsayn OOr*
16.30	sechzehn Uhr dreißig	*zesh-tsayn OOr drysish*
at half past five	um halb sechs	*oom halp zex*

HOTELS

Hotels in Germany are categorized by the international star-rating system, with the range of services and level of luxury corresponding to what you would expect to find at home. If you're looking for simpler accommodation, you could try a **Gasthof**, **Gasthaus** or **Pension**. A **Gasthof** or **Gasthaus** will often be an establishment with a restaurant on the ground floor and rooms on the other floors – a traditional inn. The signs **'Zimmer frei'** or **'Fremdenzimmer'** mean that rooms are available and, if on display in the window of a private house, will indicate a bed and breakfast type of accommodation.

USEFUL WORDS AND PHRASES

balcony	der Balkon	*balkong*
bath *(tub)*	die Badewanne	*bahduh-vannuh*
bathroom	das Bad	*baht*
bed	das Bett	*bet*
bed and breakfast	Übernachtung mit Frühstück	*mbernaKHtoong mit frmshtmk*
bedroom	das (Schlaf)zimmer	*(shlahf)tsimmer*
bill	die Rechnung	*reshnoong*
breakfast	das Frühstück	*frmshtmk*
car park	der Parkplatz	*parkplats*
dining room	der Speiseraum	*shpyzuh-rowm*
dinner *(evening)*	das Abendessen	*ahbentessen*
double bed	das Doppelbett	*doppelbet*
double room	das Doppelzimmer	*doppeltsimmer*
foyer	das Foyer	*fwa-yay*
full board	Vollpension	*follpangz-yohn*
guesthouse	die Pension	*pangz-yohn*
half board	Halbpension	*halp-pangz-yohn*
hotel	das Hotel	*hotel*
key	der Schlüssel	*shlmssel*

lift	der Aufzug, der Lift	_owf-tsOOk, lift_
lounge	die Lounge	_'lounge'_
lunch	das Mittagessen	_mittahkessen_
maid	das Zimmermädchen	_tsimmer-maydshen_
manager	der Geschäftsführer	_gushefts-fœrer_
receipt	die Quittung	_kvittoong_
reception	der Empfang	_empfang_
receptionist	der Empfangschef	_empfangs-shef_
(woman)	die Empfangsdame	_empfangs-dahmuh_
room	das Zimmer	_tsimmer_
room service	der Zimmerservice	_tsimmer-'service'_
shower	die Dusche	_dOOshuh_
single bed	das Einzelbett	_ine-tselbet_
single room	das Einzelzimmer	_ine-tsel-tsimmer_
toilet	die Toilette	_twalettuh_
twin room	das Zweibettzimmer	_tsvybet-tsimmer_
washbasin	das Waschbecken	_vashbecken_

Have you any vacancies?
Haben Sie Zimmer frei?
hahben zee tsimmer fry

I have a reservation
Ich habe ein Zimmer reserviert
ish hahbuh ine tsimmer rezerveert

I'd like a single room
Ich möchte ein Einzelzimmer
ish murshtuh ine ine-tsel-tsimmer

I'd like a room with a bathroom/balcony
Ich möchte ein Zimmer mit Bad/Balkon
ish murshtuh ine tsimmer mit baht/balkong

I'd like a room for one night/three nights
Ich möchte ein Zimmer für eine Nacht/drei Nächte
ish murshtuh ine tsimmer fœr ine-uh naKHt/dry neshtuh

What is the charge per night?
Was kostet es pro Nacht?
vass kostet ess pro naKHt

I don't know yet how long I'll stay
Ich weiß noch nicht, wie lange ich bleiben werde
ish vice noKH nisht vee lang-uh ish blyben vairduh

When is breakfast/dinner?
Wann wird das Frühstück/Abendessen serviert?
vann veert dass frwhshtwk/ahbentessen zairveert

Please wake/call me at 7 o'clock
Bitte wecken Sie mich um 7 Uhr
bittuh vecken zee mish oom zeeben OOr

Can I have breakfast in my room?
Können Sie mir das Frühstück auf mein Zimmer bringen?
kurnen zee meer dass frwshtwk owf mine tsimmer bring-en

I'll be back at 10 o'clock
Ich bin um 10 Uhr wieder da
ish bin oom tsayn OOr veeder da

My room number is 205
Meine Zimmernummer ist 205
mine-uh tsimmer-noommer ist tsvy-hoondert fwnf

I'd like to have some laundry done
Ich möchte gern meine Wäsche waschen lassen
ish murshtuh gairn mine-uh veshuh vashen lassen

My booking was for a double room
Ich hatte ein Doppelzimmer reserviert
ish hattuh ine doppeltsimmer rezerveert

I asked for a room with an en-suite bathroom
Ich hatte um ein Zimmer mit eigenem Bad gebeten
ish hattuh oom ine tsimmer mit ige-enem baht gubayten

25

I need a light bulb
Ich brauche eine Glühbirne
ish bro<u>w</u>KHuh <u>ine</u>-uh gl<u>@</u>beernuh

The lamp is broken
Die Lampe ist kaputt
dee l<u>a</u>mpuh ist kap<u>oo</u>t

There is no toilet paper in the bathroom
Im Badezimmer ist kein Toilettenpapier
im b<u>ah</u>duh-tsimmer ist kine twal<u>e</u>tten-papeer

The window won't open
Das Fenster geht nicht auf
dass f<u>e</u>nster gayt nisht owf

There isn't any hot water
Es gibt kein warmes Wasser
ess ge<u>e</u>pt kine v<u>a</u>rmess v<u>a</u>sser

The socket in the bathroom doesn't work
Die Steckdose im Badezimmer funktioniert nicht
dee sht<u>e</u>k-dohzuh im b<u>ah</u>duh-tsimmer foonkts-yon<u>ee</u>rt nisht

I'm leaving tomorrow
Ich reise morgen ab
ish r<u>y</u>zuh m<u>o</u>rgen ap

When do I have to vacate the room?
Bis wann muß ich das Zimmer räumen?
biss van mooss ish dass ts<u>i</u>mmer r<u>oy</u>men

Can I have the bill please?
Kann ich bitte die Rechnung haben?
kan ish b<u>i</u>ttuh dee r<u>e</u>shnoong h<u>ah</u>ben

I'll pay by credit card
Ich zahle mit Kreditkarte
ish ts<u>ah</u>luh mit kred<u>ee</u>tkartuh

I'll pay cash
Ich zahle in bar
ish ts<u>ah</u>luh in bar

Can you get me a taxi?
Können Sie mir ein Taxi bestellen?
k<u>ur</u>nen zee meer ine t<u>a</u>xi busht<u>e</u>llen

Can you recommend another hotel?
Können Sie ein anderes Hotel empfehlen?
k<u>ur</u>nen zee ine <u>a</u>nderess hot<u>e</u>l empf<u>ay</u>len

---

THINGS YOU'LL SEE

Aufzug	lift
Bad	bath
belegt	no vacancies
Doppelzimmer	double room
drücken	push
Dusche	shower
Eingang	entrance
Einzelzimmer	single room
Empfang	reception
Erdgeschoß	ground floor
erster Stock	first floor
Fahrstuhl	lift
Fremdenzimmer	room(s) to let
Frühstück	breakfast
Gasthaus, Gasthof	inn
Halbpension	half board
kein Zutritt	no admission
Mittagessen	lunch
Notausgang	emergency exit
nur für Gäste	patrons only
Parkplatz	car park
Pension	guesthouse

→

27

Rechnung	bill
Speisesaal	restaurant, dining room
Treppe	stairs
Übernachtung	night
Übernachtung mit Frühstück	bed and breakfast
voll belegt	no vacancies
Vollpension	full board
ziehen	pull
Zimmer frei	room(s) to let
Zuschlag	supplement
Zweibettzimmer	twin room
zweiter Stock	second floor

THINGS YOU'LL HEAR

Mit oder ohne Bad?
With or without bath?

Tut mir leid, wir sind voll belegt
I'm sorry, we're full

Es sind keine Einzelzimmer/Doppelzimmer mehr frei
There are no single/double rooms left

Für wie lange?
For how long?

Wie möchten Sie bezahlen?
How would you like to pay?

Könnten Sie bitte im voraus bezahlen
Could you please pay in advance

Sie müssen das Zimmer bis zwölf Uhr räumen
You must vacate the room by midday

CAMPING AND CARAVANNING

Germany has well over 2,500 well-equipped campsites, most of which are open from May until September. In some winter sports areas you will find sites open all year round.

There are also more than 600 youth hostels throughout the country, and mountain shelters or **Berghütten** *bairk-hʊtten* provided by hiking clubs, who also mark the more interesting trails.

USEFUL WORDS AND PHRASES

bucket	der Eimer	*ime-er*
campfire	das Lagerfeuer	*lahger-foy-er*
go camping	zelten gehen	*tselten gay-en*
campsite	der Campingplatz	*kemping-plats*
caravan	der Wohnwagen	*vohn-vahgen*
caravan site	der Wohnwagenplatz	*vohn-vahgen-plats*
cooking utensils	die Kochgeräte	*koKH-guraytuh*
drinking water	das Trinkwasser	*trinkvasser*
ground sheet	die Zeltbodenplane	*tseltbohden-plahnuh*
hitch-hike	trampen	*trempen*
rope	das Seil	*zile*
rubbish	der Abfall	*apfal*
rucksack	der Rucksack	*rookzak*
saucepans	das Kochgeschirr	*koKH-gusheer*
sleeping bag	der Schlafsack	*shlahfzak*
tent	das Zelt	*tselt*
youth hostel	die Jugendherberge	*yOOgent-hairbairguh*

Can I camp here?
Kann man hier zelten?
kan man heer tselten

Can we park the caravan here?
Können wir den Wohnwagen hier abstellen?
kurnen veer dayn vohn-vahgen heer apshtellen

Where is the nearest campsite/caravan site?
Wo ist der nächste Campingplatz/Wohnwagenplatz?
vo ist dair naykstuh kemping-plats/vohn-vahgen-plats

What is the charge per night?
Was kostet es pro Nacht?
vass kostet ess pro naKHt

How much is it for a week?
Was ist der Preis für eine Woche?
vass ist dair price fœr ine-uh voKHuh

I only want to stay for one night
Ich möchte nur eine Nacht bleiben
ish murshtuh nOOr ine-uh naKHt blyben

We're leaving tomorrow
Wir fahren morgen ab
veer faren morgen ap

Where is the kitchen?
Wo ist die Küche?
vo ist dee kœshuh

Can I light a fire here?
Kann man hier ein Feuer machen?
kan man heer ine foy-er maKHen

Where can I get ...?
Wo bekomme ich ...?
vo bukommuh ish

Is there drinking water here?
Gibt es hier Trinkwasser?
geept ess heer trinkvasser

THINGS YOU'LL SEE

Anhänger	trailer
Ausweis	pass, identity card
Benutzung	use
Bettdecken	bedding
Campingplatz	campsite
Dusche	shower
Feuer	fire
Gebühren	charges
Jugendherberge	youth hostel
Küche	kitchen
Licht	light
Schlafraum	dormitory
Schlafsäcke	sleeping bags
Trinkwasser	drinking water
Wohnwagen	caravan
Zelt	tent
Zelten verboten	no camping
Zeltplatz	campsite
zu verleihen	for hire
zu vermieten	to rent

VILLAS AND APARTMENTS

You may be asked to pay for certain "extras" not included in the original price. You might want to ask if electricity, gas etc is included. It's a good idea to ask about an inventory at the start, rather than be told something is missing later just as you are about to leave. You may be asked for a deposit – so make sure you get a receipt for this.

USEFUL WORDS AND PHRASES

agent	der Vertreter	*fairtrayter*
bath	das Bad	*baht*
bathroom	das Badezimmer	*bahduhtsimmer*
bedroom	das Zimmer	*tsimmer*
blind	das Rollo	*rollo*
blocked	verstopft	*fairshtopft*
boiler	der Boiler	*'boiler'*
break *(something)*	zerbrechen	*tsairbreshen*
broken	kaputt	*kapoot*
caretaker	der Hausmeister	*howss-myster*
central heating	die Zentralheizung	*tsentrahl-hytsoong*
cleaner	die Putzfrau	*pootsfrow*
cooker	der Herd	*hairt*
deposit	die Anzahlung	*antsahloong*
drain	der Abfluß	*apflooss*
dustbin	die Mülltonne	*maltonnuh*
electrician	der Elektriker	*aylektriker*
electricity	der Strom	*shtrohm*
fridge	der Kühlschrank	*kalshrank*
fusebox	der Sicherungskasten	*zisheroongskasten*
gas	das Gas	*gahss*
grill	der Grill	*grill*
heater	das Heizgerät	*hytsgurayt*
iron	das Bügeleisen	*bagel-ize-en*

32

ironing board	das Bügelbrett	*bügelbret*
keys	die Schlüssel	*shlüssel*
kitchen	die Küche	*küshuh*
leak	die undichte Stelle	*oondishtuh shtelluh*
light	das Licht	*lisht*
light bulb	die Glühbirne	*glübeernuh*
living room	das Wohnzimmer	*vohntsimmer*
maid	die Hausangestellte	*howss-angushtelltuh*
pillow	das Kopfkissen	*kopfkissen*
pillow slip	der Kopfkissenbezug	*kopfkissenbutsOOk*
plumber	der Klempner	*klempner*
receipt	die Quittung	*kvittoong*
refund	die Rückerstattung	*rükairshtattoong*
sheets	die Bettlaken	*bet-lahken*
shower	die Dusche	*dOOshuh*
sink	die Spüle	*shpüluh*
stopcock	der Absperrhahn	*apshpairhahn*
swimming pool	der Swimmingpool	*'swimming pool'*
tap	der Hahn	*hahn*
toilet	die Toilette	*twalettuh*
towel	das Handtuch	*hant-tOOKH*
washing machine	die Waschmaschine	*vash-masheenuh*
water	das Wasser	*vasser*
water heater	das Heißwassergerät	*hice-vassergurayt*

Does the price include gas/electricity/cleaning?
Ist der Preis einschließlich Gas/Strom/Reinigung?
ist dair price ine-shleesslish gahss/shtrohm/rynigoong

Do I need to sign an inventory?
Muß ich eine Bestandsliste unterschreiben?
mooss ish ine-uh bushtants-listuh oontershryben

Where is this item?
Wo ist dies?
vo ist deess

33

Please take it off the inventory
Bitte streichen Sie es von der Bestandsliste
bittuh shtryshen zee ess fon dair bushtants-listuh

We've broken this
Dies ist uns kaputtgegangen
deess ist oonss kapoot-gugang-en

This was broken when we arrived
Es war schon kaputt, als wir ankamen
ess var shohn kapoot alss veer ankahmen

This was missing when we arrived
Dies fehlte schon, als wir ankamen
deess fayltuh shohn alss veer ankahmen

Can I have my deposit back?
Kann ich meine Anzahlung zurückbekommen?
kan ish mine-uh antsahloong tsoorwk-bukommen

Can we have an extra bed?
Können wir ein zusätzliches Bett bekommen?
kurnen veer ine tsOOzetslishess bett bukommen

Can we have more crockery/cutlery?
Können wir mehr Geschirr/Besteck bekommen?
kurnen veer mair gusheer/bushtek bukommen

Where is ...?
Wo ist ...?
vo ist

When does the maid come?
Wann kommt die Hausangestellte?
van kommt dee howss-angushtelltuh

Where can I buy/find ...?
Wo kann ich ... kaufen/finden?
vo kan ish ... kowfen/finden

When is the bank/supermarket open?
Wann hat die Bank/der Supermarkt geöffnet?
van hat dee bank/dair zoopermarkt guh-urfnet

How does the water heater work?
Wie funktioniert das Heißwassergerät?
vee foonkts-yoneert dass hice-vassergurayt

Do you do ironing/baby-sitting?
Haben Sie einen Bügeldienst/Babysitterdienst?
hahben zee ine-en bewgeldeenst/'babysitter'-deenst

Do you prepare lunch/dinner?
Können Sie für uns mittags/abends kochen?
kurnen zee fewr oonss mittahks/ahbents koKHen

Do we have to pay extra or is this included in the price?
Ist das extra oder im Preis inbegriffen?
ist dass extra ohder im price inbugriffen

The shower doesn't work
Die Dusche funktioniert nicht
dee dOOshuh foonkts-yoneert nisht

The sink is blocked
Der Abfluß ist verstopft
dair apflooss ist fairshtopft

The sink/toilet is leaking
Der Abfluß/die Toilette leckt
dair apflooss/dee twalettuh lekt

There's a burst pipe
Ein Rohr ist geplatzt
ine ror ist guplatst

The rubbish has not been collected for a week
Der Müll ist seit einer Woche nicht abgeholt worden
dair mewl ist zite ine-er voKHuh nisht apguhohlt vorden

There's no electricity/gas/water
Es gibt keinen Strom/kein Gas/kein Wasser
ess geept kine-en shtrohm/kine gahss/kine vasser

Our bottled gas has run out – how do we get a new cylinder?
Unsere Gasflasche ist leer – wo bekommen wir eine neue?
oonzeruh gahss-flashuh ist lair vo bukommen veer ine-uh noyuh

Can you mend it today?
Können Sie es heute reparieren lassen?
kurnen zee ess hoytuh repareeren lassen

What is the name and telephone number of the nearest doctor/dentist?
Was ist der Name und die Telefonnummer des nächsten Arztes/Zahnarztes?
vass ist dair nahmuh oont dee telefohn-noommer des nayksten artstess/tsahn-artstess

Send your bill to ...
Schicken Sie die Rechnung an ...
shicken zee dee reshnoong an

I'm staying at ...
Ich wohne in ...
ish vohnuh in

Thanks for looking after us so well
Vielen Dank, daß Sie sich so gut um uns gekümmert haben
feelen dank dass zee zish zo gOOt oom oonss guk@mmert hahben

See you again next year
Bis nächstes Jahr
biss naykstess yar

MOTORING

Drive on the right, overtake on the left. On dual-lane highways you may remain in the left-hand lane if there is dense traffic on your right, but when lines of traffic have formed in all lanes you are allowed to drive faster in a right-hand lane. If you happen to be in a left-hand lane you may move to the right only in order to turn off, stop or follow directional arrows.

Traffic coming from the right has priority at crossroads and junctions wherever there is no priority sign or traffic light, unless entering the main road from a car park, service station, private road, path or forest track. Your right of way is signalled by a yellow diamond or the more familiar arrow inside a red triangle. The former gives you priority for some distance ahead while the latter applies to the next intersection only. An inverted red triangle or an octagonal STOP sign denotes that you must give way.

In built-up areas a speed limit of 50 kph (31 mph) is shown by the town's name on a yellow plate. The same plate with a diagonal red stripe marks the end of both limit and area. On other roads, except dual-lane highways, there is a speed limit of 100 kph (62 mph). Heavier vehicles – trucks or lorries, buses, cars towing caravans or trailers – are restricted to 80 kph (50 mph) on all roads and autobahns. There is no speed limit on the autobahns for cars (with the exception of some roads in what used to be East Germany).

It is illegal to drive on sidelights. Motorcyclists must use dipped headlights at all times.

SOME COMMON ROAD SIGNS

Achtung	watch out
Anlieger frei	residents only
Autobahn	motorway
Autobahndreieck	motorway junction

→

Autobahnkreuz	motorway junction
Bahnübergang	level crossing
Baustelle	roadworks
bei Frost Glatteisgefahr	icy in cold weather
bitte einordnen	get in lane
Bundesautobahn	federal motorway
Bundesstraße	A-road, trunk road
Durchgangsverkehr	through traffic
Einbahnstraße	one-way street
eingeschränktes Halteverbot	restricted parking
Fahrradweg	cycle path
Frostschäden	frost damage
Fußgänger	pedestrians
Fußgängerzone	pedestrian precinct
Gefahr	danger
gefährliche Einmündung	dangerous junction
gefährliche Kurve	dangerous bend
Gegenverkehr hat Vorfahrt	oncoming traffic has right of way
gesperrt für Fahrzeuge aller Art	closed to all vehicles
Glatteis	black ice
Halteverbot	no stopping
Höchstgeschwindigkeit	maximum speed
keine Zufahrt	no entry
Kreuzung	crossroads
Kriechspur	crawler lane
kurvenreiche Strecke	bends
Landstraße	A-road, B-road
langsam fahren	drive slowly
Nebel	fog
nur für Busse	buses only
Parken nur mit Parkscheibe	parking disc holders only

→

Parkverbot	no parking
Radweg kreuzt	cycle track crossing
Raststätte	services area
rechts fahren	keep to the right
Sackgasse	no through road
schlechte Fahrbahn	bad surface
Schule	school
Schwerlastverkehr	heavy vehicles
Seitenstreifen nicht befahrbar	soft verges
Stadtmitte	town centre
starkes Gefälle	steep gradient
Stau	tailback, traffic jam
Steinschlag	falling rocks
Straßenbahn	tram
Überholen verboten	no overtaking
Umgehungsstraße	by-pass
Umleitung	diversion
Unebenheiten	uneven surface
verengte Fahrbahn	road narrows
Vorfahrt gewähren	give way
Vorfahrtsstraße	drivers on this road have priority
Zoll	customs

USEFUL WORDS AND PHRASES

bonnet	die Motorhaube	*mohtorhowbuh*
boot	der Kofferraum	*kofferrowm*
brake	die Bremse	*bremzuh*
breakdown	die Panne	*pannuh*
car	das Auto	*owto*
car park	der Parkplatz	*parkplats*
(multistorey)	das Parkhaus	*parkhowss*
caravan	der Wohnwagen	*vohn-vahgen*

39

clutch	die Kupplung	*kooploong*
crossroads	die Kreuzung	*kroytsoong*
drive	fahren	*faren*
engine	der Motor	*mohtor*
exhaust	der Auspuff	*owss-poof*
fanbelt	der Keilriemen	*kile-reemen*
garage *(for repairs)*	die Werkstatt	*vairkshtat*
(for petrol)	die Tankstelle	*tankshtelluh*
gear	der Gang	*gang*
gears/gear box	das Getriebe	*gutreebuh*
headlights	die Scheinwerfer	*shine-vairfer*
indicator	der Blinker	*blinker*
junction	die Kreuzung	*kroytsoong*
(motorway entry)	die Auffahrt	*owf-fart*
(motorway exit)	die Ausfahrt	*owss-fart*
licence	der Führerschein	*fwrer-shine*
lorry	der Lastwagen	*last-vahgen*
mirror	der Spiegel	*shpeegel*
motorbike	das Motorrad	*motor-raht*
motorway	die Autobahn	*owtoh-bahn*
number plate	das Nummernschild	*noommern-shilt*
parking meter	die Parkuhr	*park-OOr*
parking ticket	der Strafzettel	*shtrahf-tsettel*
petrol	das Benzin	*bentseen*
petrol station	die Tankstelle	*tankshtelluh*
rear lights	das Rücklicht	*rwklisht*
road	die Straße	*shtrahssuh*
spares	die Ersatzteile	*airzats-tile-uh*
spark plug	die Zündkerze	*ts@nt-kairtsuh*
speed	die Geschwindigkeit	*gushvindish-kite*
speed limit	die Geschwindigkeits-beschränkung	*gushvindish-kites-bushrenkoong*
speedometer	der Tacho(meter)	*taKHo(mayter)*
steering wheel	das Lenkrad	*lenkraht*
tow	abschleppen	*apshleppen*
traffic lights	die Ampel	*ampel*
trailer	der Anhänger	*anheng-er*

tyre	der Reifen	*rife-en*
van	der Lieferwagen	*leefer-vahgen*
wheel	das Rad	*raht*
windscreen	die Windschutz-scheibe	*vint-shoots-shybuh*
windscreen wiper	der Scheibenwischer	*shyben-visher*

I'd like some petrol/oil/water
Ich brauche etwas Benzin/Öl/Wasser
ish browKHuh etvass bentseen/url/vasser

Fill her up please!
Volltanken bitte!
folltanken bittuh

20 litres of 4-star unleaded please
Zwanzig Liter Super bleifrei bitte
tsvantsish leeter zOOper bly-fry bittuh

Would you check the tyres please?
Könnten Sie bitte die Reifen überprüfen?
kurnten zee bittuh dee rife-en ɷberprɷfen

Do you do repairs?
Machen Sie Reparaturen?
maKHen zee reparatOOren

Can you repair the clutch?
Können Sie die Kupplung reparieren?
kurnen zee dee kooploong repareeren

There is something wrong with the engine
Mit dem Motor stimmt etwas nicht
mit daym mohtor shtimmt etvass nisht

The engine is overheating
Der Motor ist heißgelaufen
dair mohtor ist hice-gulowfen

I need a new tyre
Ich brauche einen neuen Reifen
ish browKHuh ine-en noyen rife-en

Can you replace this?
Haben Sie hierfür einen Ersatz?
hahben zee heerfur ine-en airsats

The indicator is not working
Der Blinker funktioniert nicht
dair blinker foonkts-yoneert nisht

How long will it take?
Wie lange wird das dauern?
vee lang-uh veert dass dowern

Where can I park?
Wo kann ich parken?
vo kan ish parken

Can I park here?
Kann ich hier parken?
kan ish heer parken

I'd like to hire a car
Ich möchte ein Auto mieten
ish murshtuh ine owto meeten

I'd like an automatic/a manual
Ich möchte ein Auto mit Automatik/mit Schaltung von Hand
ish murshtuh ine owto mit owtomahtik/mit shaltoong fon hant

For one day/two days/one week
Für einen Tag/zwei Tage/eine Woche
fur ine-en tahk/tsvy tahguh/ine-uh voKHuh

How much is it for one day?
Was kostet es pro Tag?
vass kostet ess pro tahk

Is there a mileage charge?
Wird ein Preis pro Kilometer erhoben?
veert ine price pro kilomayter airhohben

When do I have to return it?
Wann muß ich es wieder zurückbringen?
van mooss ish ess veeder tsoor@kbring-en

Where is the nearest petrol station?
Wo ist die nächste Tankstelle?
vo ist dee naykstuh tankshtelluh

How do I get to Fechenheim/Steinstraße?
Wie komme ich nach Fechenheim/zur Steinstraße?
vee kommuh ish nahKH feshenhime/tsOOr shtine-shtrahssuh

Is this the road to Munich?
Ist dies die Straße nach München?
ist deess dee shtrahssuh nahKH m@nshen

Which is the quickest way to Central Station?
Was ist der schnellste Weg zum Hauptbahnhof?
vass ist dair shnelstuh vayk tsoom howpt-bahnhohf

DIRECTIONS YOU MAY BE GIVEN

an der nächsten Ausfahrt	at the next junction
an der nächsten Kreuzung	at the next crossroads
erste Straße rechts	first on the right
geradeaus	straight on
links	on the left
links abbiegen	turn left
rechts	on the right
rechts abbiegen	turn right
vorbei an ...	past the ...
zweite Straße links	second on the left

43

THINGS YOU'LL SEE

Ausfahrt	exit
Autowäsche	car wash
Benzin	petrol
bleifrei	leadfree
Bremsflüssigkeit	brake fluid
Einfahrt	entrance, way in
Geschwindigkeits-beschränkung	speed limit
LKW	heavy goods vehicle, HGV
Luftdruck	air pressure
Motor abstellen	switch off engine
Münztank	coin-operated pump
Normal(benzin)	2-star
Öl	oil
Parkhaus	multistorey car park
Parkplatz	car park
Parkschein entnehmen	take a ticket
PKW	private car
Reifendruck	tyre pressure
Reparaturwerkstatt	garage, repairs
Schritt fahren	drive at walking speed
Super	4-star
Tankstelle	petrol station
unverbleit	unleaded
verbleit	leaded
Waschstraße	car wash
Wasser	water
Zapfsäule	petrol pump

YOU MAY HEAR

Kann ich bitte Ihren Führerschein sehen?
May I see your driving licence please?

TRAVELLING AROUND

AIR TRAVEL

In addition to an excellent domestic network, air services connect the following German cities with many UK and USA destinations: Berlin, Bremen, Cologne (**Köln**)/Bonn, Düsseldorf, Frankfurt am Main, Hamburg, Hanover, Leipzig, Munich (**München**), Nuremberg (**Nürnberg**) and Stuttgart.

RAIL TRAVEL

The German Federal Railways or **DB** (**Deutsche Bundesbahn**) are outstanding for their punctuality and general efficiency. International trains connect Germany with most parts of Europe, while fast, regular Inter-City and express trains link the larger German towns and cities. The main types of train are:

TEE	Trans European Express
IC	Inter-City
D	Express
E(Eilzug)	Semi-fast train
Personenzug	Local train - stopping at every station

A supplement or **Zuschlag** *tsOOshlahk* is payable for all journeys by **TEE** and **IC** trains and on some **D** trains for journeys under 50 kms.

LOCAL TRANSPORT, BOAT TRAVEL

There are good bus and tram networks in all German towns and cities. Single tickets can be bought from a ticket machine located by the bus or tram stop or sometimes from the driver. It is usually cheaper to buy a multi-journey ticket from a ticket machine. If you need to change buses or trams en route it is not necessary to buy another ticket. In some cities you will also have to stamp your ticket in a ticket-stamping machine situated on board the bus or tram – you will have to do this if you have bought a multi-journey ticket.

Some of the larger cities such as Hamburg, Munich, Berlin, Frankfurt, Cologne and Nuremberg have an underground system or **U-Bahn** _OObahn_ and some cities also have a fast local rail network or **S-Bahn** _ess-bahn_. Zone systems also operate in major cities, a flat fare applying in each zone with the fare increasing according to the number of zones crossed. Tickets can be obtained from automatic ticket machines, most of which give change.

A number of rural bus services are also run by the German Federal Railways and Federal Post. Post buses are yellow, while those belonging to the Federal Railways are red.

A more leisurely way of travelling in Germany, especially during the summer months, is on one of the steamer services operated on the major rivers such as the Rhine (**der Rhein**), Moselle (**die Mosel** _mohzel_) and Danube (**die Donau** _dohnow_) and on Lake Constance (**der Bodensee** _bohdenzay_), the Bavarian lakes and the Berlin lakes.

TAXIS

Taxis are normally hired from a taxi rank or by telephone. It is not customary in Germany to hail a taxi on the street.

USEFUL WORDS AND PHRASES

airport	der Flughafen	_flOOk-hahfen_
airport bus	der Flughafenbus	_flOOk-hahfenbooss_
aisle seat	der Sitz am Gang	_sits am gang_
adult	der Erwachsene	_airvaksenuh_
baggage claim	die Gepäckausgabe	_gupek-owssgahbuh_
boarding card	die Bordkarte	_bort-kartuh_
boat	das Schiff	_shiff_
booking office	der Fahrkarten- schalter	_farkarten-shalter_
bus	der Bus	_booss_
bus station	der Busbahnhof	_boossbahnhohf_
bus stop	die Bushaltestelle	_booss-haltuh-shtelluh_
carriage	der Wagen	_vahgen_

check-in desk	der Abfertigungs-schalter	*apfairtigoongs-shalter*
child	das Kind	*kint*
coach *(bus)*	der Bus	*booss*
compartment	das Abteil	*aptile*
connection	die Verbindung	*fairbindoong*
cruise	die Kreuzfahrt	*kroyts-fart*
Customs	der Zoll	*tsoll*
departure lounge	die Abflughalle	*apflOOk-halluh*
domestic	Inland-	*inlant-*
emergency exit	der Notausgang	*noht-owssgang*
(on plane)	der Notausstieg	*noht-owss-shteek*
entrance	der Eingang	*ine-gang*
exit	der Ausgang	*owssgang*
fare	der Fahrpreis	*farprice*
ferry	die Fähre	*fayruh*
first class	die erste Klasse	*airstuh klassuh*
flight	der Flug	*flOOk*
flight number	die Flugnummer	*flOOknoommer*
gate	der Flugsteig	*flOOk-shtike*
hand luggage	das Handgepäck	*hant-gupek*
international	international	*internats-yonahl*
left luggage office	die Gepäck-aufbewahrung	*gupek-owfbuvaroong*
lost property office	das Fundbüro	*foont-büro*
luggage trolley	der Kofferkuli	*kofferkOOlee*
network map	der Netzplan	*netsplahn*
non-smoking	Nichtraucher	*nishtrowKHer*
number 5 bus	der Bus Nr. 5	*booss noommer fünf*
passport	der Paß	*pas*
platform	der Bahnsteig	*bahn-shtike*
railway	die Eisenbahn	*ize-en-bahn*
reserved seat	der reservierte Platz	*rezerveertuh plats*
restaurant car	der Speisewagen	*shpyzuh-vahgen*
return ticket	die Rückfahrkarte	*rükfarkartuh*

47

seat	der Platz	*plats*
second class	die zweite Klasse	*tsvytuh klassuh*
single ticket	die einfache Fahrkarte	*ine-faKHuh farkartuh*
sleeper	der Schlafwagen	*shlahf-vahgen*
smoking	Raucher	*rowKHer*
station	der Bahnhof	*bahnhohf*
taxi	das Taxi	*taxi*
terminus	die Endstation	*ent-shtats-yohn*
ticket	die Fahrkarte	*farkartuh*
(air)	das Ticket	*'ticket'*
timetable	der Fahrplan	*farplahn*
train	der Zug	*tsOOk*
tram	die Straßenbahn	*shtrahssenbahn*
underground	die U-Bahn	*OObahn*
waiting room	der Wartesaal	*vartuh-zahl*
window seat	der Fensterplatz	*fensterplats*

AIR TRAVEL

I'd like a non-smoking seat please
Ich möchte gern einen Nichtraucherplatz
ish murshtuh gairn ine-en nisht-rowKHerplats

I'd like a window seat please
Ich möchte gern einen Fensterplatz
ish murshtuh gairn ine-en fensterplats

How long will the flight be delayed?
Wie lange wird die Verzögerung dauern?
vee lang-uh veert dee fairtsurgeroong dowern

Which gate for the flight to Heathrow?
Von welchem Flugsteig fliegt die Maschine nach Heathrow?
fon velshem flOOk-shtike fleekt dee masheenuh nahKH 'heathrow'

RAIL, BUS AND UNDERGROUND TRAVEL

When does the train/bus for Frankfurt leave?
Wann fährt der Zug/Bus nach Frankfurt ab?
van fairt dair tsOOk/booss nahKH frankfoort ap

When does the train/bus from Munich arrive?
Wann kommt der Zug/Bus aus München an?
van kommt dair tsOOk/booss owss munshen an

When is the next train/bus to Nuremberg?
Wann fährt der nächste Zug/Bus nach Nürnberg?
van fairt dair naykstuh tsOOk/booss nahKH nurnbairk

When is the first train/bus to Pforzheim?
Wann fährt der erste Zug/Bus nach Pforzheim?
van fairt dair airstuh tsOOk/booss nahKH pforts-hime

When is the last train/bus to Cologne?
Wann fährt der letzte Zug/Bus nach Köln?
van fayrt dair letstuh tsOOk/booss nahKH kurln

What is the fare to Heidelberg?
Was kostet die Fahrt nach Heidelberg?
vass kostet dee fart nahKH hydelbairk

Do I have to change?
Muß ich umsteigen?
mooss ish oomshtygen

Does the train/bus stop at Lüneburg?
Hält der Zug/Bus in Lüneburg?
helt dair tsOOk/booss in lunuh-boork

How long does it take to get to Dresden?
Wie lange dauert die Fahrt nach Dresden?
vee lang-uh dowert dee fart nahKH draysden

Where can I buy a ticket?
Wo kann ich eine Fahrkarte lösen?
vo kan ish ine-uh farkartuh lurzen

A single/return ticket to Bremen please
Eine einfache Fahrkarte/eine Rückfahrkarte nach Bremen, bitte
*ine-uh ine-faKHuh farkartuh/ine-uh ruckfarkartuh nahKH
braymen bittuh*

Could you help me get a ticket?
Könnten Sie mir bitte helfen, eine Fahrkarte zu lösen?
kurnten zee meer bittuh helfen ine-uh farkartuh tsoo lurzen

Do I have to pay a supplement?
Muß ich einen Zuschlag zahlen?
mooss ish ine-en tsOOshlahk tsahlen

I'd like to reserve a seat
Ich möchte gern einen Platz reservieren
ish murshtuh gairn ine-en plats rezerveeren

Is this the right train/bus for Bonn?
Ist dies der Zug/Bus nach Bonn?
ist deess dair tsOOk/booss nahKH bon

Is this the right platform for the Wiesbaden train?
Ist dies das Gleis für den Zug nach Wiesbaden?
ist deess dass glice fur dayn tsOOk nahKH veessbahden

Which platform for the Düsseldorf train?
Von welchem Gleis fährt der Zug nach Düsseldorf?
fon velshem glice fairt dair tsOOk nahKH dusseldorf

Is the train/bus late?
Hat der Zug/Bus Verspätung?
hat dair tsOOk/booss fairshpaytoong

Could you help me with my luggage please?
Könnten Sie mir bitte mit meinem Gepäck behilflich sein?
kurnten zee meer bittuh mit mine-em gupek buhilflish zine

Is this a non-smoking compartment?
Ist dies ein Nichtraucherabteil?
ist deess ine nishtrowKHer-aptile

Is this seat free?
Ist dieser Platz frei?
ist deezer plats fry

This seat is taken
Dieser Platz ist besetzt
deezer plats ist buzetst

I have reserved this seat
Ich habe eine Reservierung für diesen Platz
ish hahbuh ine-uh rezerveeroong foor deezen plats

May I open/close the window?
Kann ich das Fenster öffnen/schließen?
kan ish dass fenster urfnen/shleessen

When do we arrive in Saarbrücken?
Wann kommen wir in Saarbrücken an?
van kommen veer in zarbr@ken an

What station is this?
Wo sind wir hier?
vo zint veer heer

Do we stop at Singen?
Halten wir in Singen?
halten veer in zing-en

Would you keep an eye on my things for a moment?
Könnten Sie bitte einen Moment auf meine Sachen aufpassen?
kurnten zee bittuh ine-en mohment owf mine-uh zaKHen owf-passen

Is there a restaurant car on this train?
Hat dieser Zug einen Speisewagen?
hat deezer tsOOk ine-en shpyzuh-vahgen

REPLIES YOU MAY BE GIVEN

Der nächste Zug fährt um neun Uhr dreißig
The next train leaves at nine thirty

Umsteigen in Darmstadt
Change at Darmstadt

Sie müssen einen Zuschlag zahlen
You have to pay a supplement

Es sind keine Plätze mehr frei
There are no more seats available

Where is the nearest underground station?
Wo ist die nächste U-Bahn-Station?
vo ist dee naykstuh OObahn-shtats-yohn

Where is the bus station?
Wo ist der Busbahnhof?
vo ist dair boossbahnhohf

Which buses go to Baden-Baden?
Welche Busse fahren nach Baden-Baden?
velshuh boossuh faren nahKH bahden-bahden

How often do the buses to Travemünde run?
Wie oft fahren die Busse nach Travemünde?
vee oft faren dee boossuh nahKH trahvuh-mᴔnduh

Will you let me know when we're there?
Sagen Sie mir bitte Bescheid, wenn wir da sind
zahgen zee meer bittuh bushite ven veer da zint

Do I have to get off here?
Muß ich hier aussteigen?
mooss ish heer owss-shtygen

How do you get to Bad Homburg?
Wie komme ich am besten nach Bad Homburg?
vee kommuh ish am besten nahKH baht homboork

I want to go to Hamelin
Ich möchte nach Hameln fahren
ish murshtuh nahKH hahmeln faren

Do you go near Wildbad?
Fahren Sie in die Nähe von Wildbad?
faren zee in dee nay-uh fon viltbaht

TAXIS

To the airport please
Zum Flughafen bitte
tsoom flOOkhahfen bittuh

How much will it cost?
Was wird das kosten?
vass veert dass kosten

Could you stop just here
Können Sie hier halten, bitte
kurnen zee heer halten bittuh

Could you wait for a moment then take me back?
Können Sie hier einen Moment warten und mich dann wieder zurückfahren?
kurnen zee heer ine-en moment varten oont mish dan veeder tsoorükfaren

THINGS YOU'LL SEE

Abfahrt	departure(s)
Abfertigung	check-in
Abflug	departure(s)
abgezähltes Geld	exact fare
Ankunft	arrival(s)
Ausgang	departure, exit
Auskunft	information
Ausland	international
außer sonntags	Sundays excepted
Ausweis	pass
Bahnhofsmission	office providing help for travellers in difficulty
Bahnhofspolizei	railway police
Bahnsteig	platform
Bahnsteigkarte	platform ticket
Behinderte	handicapped persons
besetzt	engaged
bezahlen	to pay
bitte anschnallen	fasten seat belt
Damen	ladies
DB (Deutsche Bundesbahn)	German railways
Direktflug	direct flight
einchecken	to check in
einfache Fahrt	single journey
Einstieg nur mit Fahrausweis	obtain a ticket before boarding
Einstieg vorn/hinten	entrance at front/rear
einwerfen	to insert
Endstation	terminus
Entwerter	ticket stamping machine
Erwachsene	adults
Fahrausweis	ticket

→

Fahrer	driver
Fahrgäste	passengers
Fahrkarte	ticket
Fahrkartenautomat	ticket machine
Fahrkartenschalter	tickets, ticket office
Fahrplan	timetable
Fahrschein	ticket
Fahrscheinkauf nur beim Fahrer	buy your ticket from the driver
Fahrt	journey
Flug	flight
Flugdauer	flight time
Flughafenbus	airport bus
Flugplan	timetable
Flugsteig	gate
frei	vacant
Geldeinwurf	insert money here
Geldrückgabe	returned coins
Gepäckaufbewahrung	left luggage
Gepäckausgabe	baggage claim
Gepäckschließfächer	luggage lockers
gesperrt	closed, no entry
Gleis	platform
Hafen	harbour
Hafenrundfahrt	boat trip round the harbour
hält nicht in ...	does not stop in ...
Haltestelle	stop
Hauptbahnhof (Hbf)	central station
Herren	gents
hier einsteigen	enter here
Imbiß	snacks
Inland	domestic
kein Ausstieg	no exit
kein Einstieg	exit only, enter by other door
kein Zugang	no entry

→

Kinder	children
Kurzstrecke	short distance (with a lower fare)
Linie	line, airline
Linienflug	scheduled flight
Mehrfahrtenkarte	multi-journey ticket
Mißbrauch strafbar	penalty for misuse
Monatskarte	monthly ticket
Münzen	coins
Nah(schnell)verkehrszug	local train
Netzkarte	travelcard
nicht hinauslehnen	do not lean out of the window
nicht rauchen	no smoking
Nichtraucher	non-smokers
Notausgang	emergency exit
Notausstieg	emergency exit
Notbremse	emergency brake
nur werktags	weekdays only
Ortszeit	local time
Passagiere	passengers
Paßkontrolle	passport control
Platzkarte	seat reservation
Rauchen verboten	no smoking
Raucher	smokers
Reiseauskunft	travel information
reserviert	reserved
Sammelkarte	multi-journey ticket
samstags	on Saturdays
S-Bahn	local railway system
Schlafwagen	sleeper
Schließfächer	luggage lockers
Sitzplätze	seats
sonn- und feiertags	on Sundays and public holidays
Speisewagen	restaurant car

→

Stehplätze	standing room
Strecke	route
Tageskarte	day ticket
U-Bahn	underground
U-Bahnhof	underground station
umsteigen	to change
Verspätung	delay
Wagen	carriage
Wagenstandanzeiger	order of cars
Wartesaal	waiting room
Wechselstube	currency exchange
zahlen	to pay
Zeitungen/Zeitschriften	newspapers/magazines
Zoll	customs
zu den Zügen	to the trains
zuschlagpflichtig	supplement must be paid
Zwischenlandung	intermediate stop

THINGS YOU'LL HEAR

Haben Sie Gepäck?
Have you any luggage?

Raucher oder Nichtraucher?
Smoking or non-smoking?

Fenstersitz oder Sitz am Gang?
Window seat or aisle seat?

Kann ich bitte Ihren Paß/Ihr Ticket sehen?
Can I see your passport/ticket, please?

Die Passagiere werden gebeten, sich zum Flugsteig 7 zu begeben
Passengers are requested to proceed to gate 7

→

57

Erster/letzter Aufruf für Flug BA302 nach Birmingham
First/last call for flight BA302 to Birmingham

Achtung!
Attention!

Bitte einsteigen
Board the train

Der Zug nach Lübeck hat Einfahrt nach Gleis 7
The train for Lübeck is approaching platform 7

Vorsicht bei der Einfahrt des Zuges
Please stand well clear of the approaching train

Planmäßige Ankunft: 13 Uhr 50
Scheduled arrival: 13.50

Der Zug hält nicht in Brühl
The train does not stop in Brühl

Der Zug fährt sofort ab
The train is now leaving

Der Zug hat zehn Minuten Verspätung
The train is ten minutes late

Bitte von der Bahnsteigkante zurücktreten
Please stand clear of the edge of the platform

Einsteigen und Türen schließen
Board the train and close the doors

Die Fahrkarten bitte
Tickets please

Noch jemand zugestiegen?
Any more tickets?

RESTAURANTS

In Germany you'll find as wide a range of restaurants as in any country, from the gourmet de luxe to the sausage and chips kiosk on the pavement. Fast food outlets, Chinese, Italian and Greek restaurants will be familiar. Not so perhaps the **Balkangrill**, serving spicy dishes from the Balkan countries. If you want something typically German you could do a lot worse than try a small **Gasthaus** *gast-howss* or inn. Some dishes vary from region to region, but one shared characteristic you'll find is that German portions are not skimpy. Germans tend to eat a lot of meat; vegetarians might have to make a special request.

Ask for a small beer (**ein kleines Bier** *ine kline-ess beer*) and you'll normally get a glass of around 0.2 litres. A large beer (**ein großes Bier** *ine grohss-ess beer*) will normally be 0.4 or 0.5 litres, although in Bavaria you may well get a litre, which is known as **eine Maß** *ine-uh mahss*. German beer is usually pils. In some areas you might try **Alt**, which is a darker beer. German wine is either **süß** *süss* (sweet), **trocken** *trocken* (dry) or, if you like it dry and a little sharper, **herb** *hairp*. If you'd like to try a local wine, ask for **einen Wein aus dieser Gegend** *ine-en vine owss deezer gaygent*.

If you're having a drink in a pub or bar you don't pay when ordering. Instead the barman or barmaid will keep a tally of what you've bought, often ticking it off on your beer mat. If you sit at a table, you can expect table service (for no extra price). There are no restrictions on taking children into pubs.

USEFUL WORDS AND PHRASES

beer	das Bier	*beer*
bill	die Rechnung	*reshnoong*
bottle	die Flasche	*flashuh*
bread	das Brot	*broht*
butter	die Butter	*booter*
café	das Café	*kaffay*
cake	der Kuchen	*kOOKHen*

carafe	die Karaffe	*karaffuh*
children's portion	der Kinderteller	*kinderteller*
coffee	der Kaffee	*kaffay*
cup	die Tasse	*tassuh*
dessert	das Dessert	*dessair*
fork	die Gabel	*gahbel*
glass	das Glas	*glahss*
half-litre	der halbe Liter	*halbuh leeter*
knife	das Messer	*messer*
main course	das Hauptgericht	*howpt-gurisht*
menu	die Speisekarte	*shpyzuh-kartuh*
milk	die Milch	*milsh*
pepper	der Pfeffer	*pfeffer*
plate	der Teller	*teller*
receipt	die Quittung	*kvittoong*
restaurant	das Restaurant	*restorong*
salt	das Salz	*zalts*
sandwich	das belegte Brot	*bulayktuh broht*
serviette	die Serviette	*zairvee-ettuh*
snack	der Imbiß	*imbiss*
soup	die Suppe	*zooppuh*
spoon	der Löffel	*lurfel*
starter	die Vorspeise	*forshpyzuh*
sugar	der Zucker	*tsooker*
table	der Tisch	*tish*
tea	der Tee	*tay*
teaspoon	der Teelöffel	*taylurfel*
tip	das Trinkgeld	*trinkgelt*
waiter	der Ober	*ohber*
waitress	die Bedienung	*budeenoong*
water	das Wasser	*vasser*
wine	der Wein	*vine*
wine list	die Weinkarte	*vine-kartuh*

A table for one/two/three, please

Einen Tisch für eine Person/zwei/drei Personen, bitte
ine-en tish f器 ine-uh pairzohn/tsvy/dry pairzohnen bittuh

Can I see the menu/wine list?
Könnte ich bitte die Speisekarte/Weinkarte haben?
kurntuh ish bittuh dee shpyzuh-kartuh/vine-kartuh hahben

What would you recommend?
Was könnten Sie empfehlen?
vass kurnten zee empfaylen

I'd like ...
Ich hätte gern ...
ish hettuh gairn

Just a cup of coffee, please
Nur eine Tasse Kaffee, bitte
nOOr ine-uh tassuh kaffay bittuh

I only want a snack
Ich möchte nur eine Kleinigkeit
ish murshtuh nOOr ine-uh kline-ishkite

Is there a set menu?
Gibt es ein Tagesgericht?
geept ess ine tahges-gurisht

A litre carafe of house red, please
Einen Liter roten Tafelwein, bitte
ine-en leeter rohten tahfel-vine bittuh

Do you have any vegetarian dishes?
Haben Sie vegetarische Gerichte?
hahben zee vegetarishuh gurishtuh

Could we have some water, please?
Könnten wir etwas Wasser haben, bitte?
kurnten veer etvass vasser hahben bittuh

Two more beers, please
Noch zwei Bier, bitte
noKH tsvy beer bittuh

Do you do children's portions?
Gibt es auch Kinderteller?
geept ess owKH kinderteller

Waiter/Waitress!
Herr Ober!/Fräulein!
hair ohber/froyline

We didn't order this
Das haben wir nicht bestellt
dass hahben veer nisht bushtellt

You've forgotten to bring my dessert
Sie haben mein Dessert vergessen
zee hahben mine dessair fairgessen

May we have some more ...?
Könnten wir noch etwas ... haben?
kurnten veer noKH etvass ... hahben

Can I have a different knife/fork?
Kann ich bitte ein anderes Messer/eine andere Gabel haben?
kan ish bittuh ine anderess messer/ine-uh anderuh gahbel hahben

Can we have the bill, please?
Zahlen, bitte
tsahlen bittuh

Could I have a receipt, please?
Könnte ich bitte eine Quittung bekommen?
kurntuh ish bittuh ine-uh kvittoong bukommen

Can we pay separately?
Können wir getrennt bezahlen?
kurnen veer gutrennt butsahlen

The meal was very good, thank you
Es hat sehr gut geschmeckt, vielen Dank
es hat zair gOOt gushmeckt feelen dank

My compliments to the chef!
Mein Kompliment Ihrem Koch!
mine kompliment eerem koKH

THINGS YOU'LL HEAR

Guten Appetit!
Enjoy your meal!

Was möchten Sie trinken?
What would you like to drink?

Hat es Ihnen geschmeckt?
Did you enjoy your meal?

THINGS YOU'LL SEE

Bedienung inbegriffen	service included
Bierkeller	beer cellar
Eiscafé	ice cream parlour (also serves coffee and liqueurs)
Gasthaus	inn, small restaurant, pub (sometimes with accommodation)
Gaststätte	inn, small restaurant, pub
Ratskeller	restaurant and bar close to town hall
Schnellimbiß	take-away, snack bar (no seating)
Speisekarte	menu
Tageskarte	menu of the day
Weinstube	wine bar (traditional style)
Wirtshaus	pub

MENU GUIDE

Aal	eel
Aalsuppe	eel soup
am Spieß	on the spit
Ananas	pineapple
Äpfel	apples
Apfel im Schlafrock	baked apple in puff pastry
Apfelkompott	stewed apples
Apfelmus	apple purée
Apfelsaft	apple juice
Apfelsinen	oranges
Apfelstrudel	apple strudel
Apfeltasche	apple turnover
Apfelwein	cider
Aprikosen	apricots
Arme Ritter	bread soaked in milk and egg then fried
Artischocken	artichokes
Aspik	aspic
Auberginen	aubergines
Auflauf	(baked) pudding or omelette
Aufschnitt	sliced cold meats, cold cuts
Austern	oysters
Backobst	dried fruit
Backpflaume	prune
Baiser	meringue
Balkansalat	cabbage and pepper salad
Bananen	bananas
Bandnudeln	ribbon noodles
Basilikum	basil
Bauernauflauf	bacon and potato omelette
Bauernfrühstück	bacon and potato omelette
Bauernomelett	bacon and potato omelette
Bechamelkartoffeln	sliced potatoes in creamy sauce
Bechamelsoße	creamy sauce with onions and ham
Bedienung	service
Beilagen	side dishes
Berliner (Ballen)	jam doughnut
Bier	beer

Birnen	pears
Biskuit	sponge
Biskuitrolle	Swiss roll
Bismarckhering	filleted pickled herring
Blätterteig	puff pastry
blau	boiled
Blaukraut	red cabbage
Blumenkohl	cauliflower
Blumenkohlsuppe	cauliflower soup
blutig	rare
Blutwurst	blood sausage
Bockwurst	large frankfurter
Bohnen	beans
Bohneneintopf	bean stew
Bohnensalat	bean salad
Bohnensuppe	bean soup
Bouillon	clear soup
Bouletten	meat balls
Braten	roast meat
Bratensoße	gravy
Brathering	(pickled) fried herring *(served cold)*
Bratkartoffeln	fried potatoes
Bratwurst	grilled pork sausage
Brot	bread
Brötchen	roll
Brühwurst	large frankfurter
Brust	breast
Bückling	smoked red herring
Bunte Platte	mixed platter
Burgundersoße	Burgundy wine sauce
Buttercremetorte	cream cake
Buttermilch	buttermilk
Champignons	mushrooms
Champignonsoße	mushroom sauce
Chinakohl	Chinese cabbage
Cordon bleu	veal cordon bleu
Currywurst mit Pommes frites	curried pork sausage with chips
Dampfnudeln	sweet yeast dumpling
Deutsches Beefsteak	mince patty, minced meat
Dicke Bohnen	broad beans

Dillsoße	dill sauce
durchgebraten	well-done
durchwachsen	with fat
durchwachsener Speck	streaky bacon
Eier	eggs
Eierauflauf	omelette
Eierkuchen	pancake
Eierpfannkuchen	pancake
Eierspeise	egg dish
eingelegt	pickled
Eintopf	stew
Eintopfgericht	stew
Eis	ice
Eisbecher	sundae
Eisbein	knuckles of pork
Eisschokolade	iced chocolate
Eissplittertorte	ice chip cake
Endiviensalat	endive salad
englisch	rare
Entenbraten	roast duck
entgrätet	boned
Erbsen	peas
Erbsensuppe	pea soup
Erdbeertorte	strawberry cake
Essig	vinegar
Falscher Hase	meat loaf
Fasan	pheasant
Feldsalat	lamb's lettuce
Fenchel	fennel
Fett	fat
Filet	fillet (steak)
Fisch	fish
Fischfilet	fish fillet
Fischfrikadellen	fishcakes
Fischstäbchen	fish fingers
Flädlesuppe	consommé with pancake strips
flambiert	flambéd
Fleischbrühe	bouillon
Fleischkäse	meat loaf
Fleischklößchen	meat ball(s)
Fleischpastete	meat vol-au-vent

Fleischsalat	diced meat salad with mayonnaise
Fleischwurst	pork sausage
Fond	meat juices
Forelle	trout
Forelle blau	boiled trout
Forelle Müllerin (Art)	trout with butter and lemon *(breaded)*
Frikadelle	rissole
Frikassee	fricassee
fritiert	(deep-)fried
Froschschenkel	frog's legs
Fruchtsaft	fruit juice
Frühlingsrolle	spring roll
Gabelrollmops	rolled-up pickled herring, rollmops
Gans	goose
Gänsebraten	roast goose
Gänseleber	goose liver
Gänseleberpastete	goose-liver pâté
garniert	garnished
Gebäck	pastries, cakes
gebacken	fried
gebeizt	marinaded
gebraten	roast
gebunden	thickened
gedünstet	steamed
Geflügel	poultry
Geflügelleber	chicken liver
Geflügelleberragout	chicken liver ragoût
gefüllt	stuffed
gefüllte Kalbsbrust	veal roll
gegart	cooked
gekocht	boiled
gekochter Schinken	boiled ham
Gelee	jelly
gemischter Salat	mixed salad
Gemüse	vegetable(s)
Gemüseplatte	assorted vegetables
Gemüsereis	rice with vegetables
Gemüsesalat	vegetable salad
Gemüsesuppe	vegetable soup
gepökelt	salted, pickled

geräuchert	smoked
Gericht	dish
geschmort	braised; stewed
Geschnetzeltes	strips of meat in thick sauce
Geselchtes	salted and smoked meat
gespickt	larded
Getränke	beverages
Gewürze	spices
Gewürzgurken	gherkins
Goldbarsch	type of perch
Götterspeise	jelly
gratiniert	au gratin
Grieß	semolina
Grießklößchen	semolina dumplings
Grießpudding	semolina pudding
Grießsuppe	semolina soup
grüne Bohnen	French beans
grüne Nudeln	green pasta
grüner Aal	fresh eel
Grünkohl	(curly) kale
Gulasch	goulash
Gulaschsuppe	goulash soup
Gurkensalat	cucumber salad
Hackfleisch	mince
Hähnchen	chicken
Hähnchenkeule	chicken leg
Haifischflossensuppe	shark-fin soup
Hammelbraten	roast mutton
Hammelfleisch	mutton
Hammelkeule	leg of mutton
Hammelrücken	saddle of mutton
Hartkäse	hard cheese
Haschee	hash
Hasenkeule	haunch of hare
Hasenpfeffer	jugged hare
Hauptspeisen	main courses
Hausfrauenart	home-made style
Hausmacher (Art)	home-made style
Hecht	pike
Heidelbeeren	bilberries, blueberries
Heilbutt	halibut

Heringssalat	herring salad
Heringsstipp	herring salad
Heringstopf	pickled herrings in sauce
Herz	heart
Herzragout	heart ragoût
Himbeeren	raspberries
Himmel und Erde	potato and apple purée with blood sausage or liver sausage
Hirn	brains
Hirschbraten	roast venison
Hirschmedaillons	small venison fillets
Honig	honey
Honigkuchen	honey cake
Honigmelone	honeydew melon
Hoppelpoppel	bacon and potato omelette
Hüfte	haunch
Huhn	chicken
Hühnerbrühe	chicken broth
Hühnerfrikassee	chicken fricassee
Hühnersuppe	chicken soup
Hülsenfrüchte	peas and beans, pulses
Hummer	lobster
Jägerschnitzel	cutlet with mushrooms
Kabeljau	cod
Kaffee	coffee
Kaiserschmarren	sugared pancake with raisins
Kakao	cocoa
Kalbfleisch	veal
Kalbsbraten	roast veal
Kalbsbries	sweetbread
Kalbsfrikassee	veal fricassee
Kalbshaxe	leg of veal
Kalbsmedaillons	small veal fillets
Kalbsnierenbraten	roast veal with kidney
Kalbsschnitzel	veal cutlet
kalte Platte	cold meal
kalter Braten	cold meat
kaltes Büfett	cold buffet
Kaltschale	cold sweet soup made from fruit
Kaninchen	rabbit
Kaninchenbraten	roast rabbit

Kapern	capers
Karamelpudding	caramel pudding
Karotten	carrots
Karpfen	carp
Kartoffelbrei	potato purée
Kartoffelklöße	potato dumplings
Kartoffelknödel	potato dumplings
Kartoffeln	potatoes
Kartoffelpuffer	potato fritters
Kartoffelpüree	potato purée
Kartoffelsalat	potato salad
Kartoffelsuppe	potato soup
Käse	cheese
Käse-Sahne-Torte	cream cheesecake
Käsegebäck	cheese savouries
Käsekuchen	cheesecake
Käseplatte	selection of cheeses
Käsesalat	cheese salad
Käsesoße	cheese sauce
Käsespätzle	home-made noodles with cheese
Kasseler Rippenspeer	salted rib of pork
Kasserolle	casserole
Kassler	smoked and braised pork chop
Kastanien	chestnuts
Katenrauchwurst	smoked sausage
Keule	leg, haunch
Kieler Sprotten	smoked sprats
Kirschen	cherries
klare Brühe	clear soup
Klößchensuppe	clear soup with dumplings
Klöße	dumplings
Knäckebrot	crispbread
Knacker	frankfurter(s)
Knackwurst	frankfurter
Knoblauch	garlic
Knoblauchbrot	garlic bread
Knochen	bone
Knochenschinken	ham on the bone
Knödel	dumplings
Kognak	brandy
Kohl	cabbage

Kohl und Pinkel	cabbage, potatoes, sausage and smoked meat
Kohlrabi	kohlrabi *(type of cabbage)*
Kohlrouladen	stuffed cabbage leaves
Kompott	stewed fruit
Konfitüre	jam
Königinpastete	chicken vol-au-vent
Königsberger Klopse	meatballs in caper sauce
Königskuchen	type of fruit cake
Kopfsalat	lettuce
Kotelett	chop
Krabben	shrimps; prawns
Krabbencocktail	prawn cocktail
Kraftbrühe	beef consommé
Kräuter	herbs
Kräuterbutter	herb butter
Kräuterkäse	cheese flavoured with herbs
Kräuterquark	curd cheese with herbs
Kräutersoße	herb sauce
Kräutertee	herbal tea
Krautsalat	coleslaw
Krautwickel	stuffed cabbage leaves
Krebs	crayfish
Kresse	cress
Kroketten	croquettes
Kruste	crust
Kuchen	cake
Kürbis	pumpkin
Labskaus	meat, fish and potato stew
Lachs	salmon
Lachsersatz	sliced and salted pollack *(fish)*
Lachsforelle	sea trout
Lachsschinken	smoked rolled fillet of ham
Lamm	lamb
Lammrücken	saddle of lamb
Langusten	crayfish
Lauch	leek
Leber	liver
Leberkäse	baked pork and beef loaf
Leberklöße	liver dumplings
Leberknödel	liver dumplings

71

Leberpastete	liver pâté
Leberwurst	liver pâté
Lebkuchen	type of gingerbread, often chocolate-covered
Leipziger Allerlei	mixed vegetables
Likör	liqueur
Limonade	lemonade
Linseneintopf	lentil stew
Linsensuppe	lentil soup
mager	lean
Majoran	marjoram
Makrele	mackerel
Makronen	macaroons
Mandeln	almonds
mariniert	marinaded, pickled
Markklößchen	marrow dumplings
Marmelade	jam
Marmorkuchen	marble cake
Maronen	sweet chestnuts
Matjes(hering)	young herring
Medaillons	small fillets
Meeresfische	seafish
Meeresfrüchte	seafood
Meerrettich	horseradish
Meerrettichsoße	horseradish sauce
Mehlspeise	sweet dish made with flour, milk, butter and eggs
Melone	melon
Miesmuscheln	mussels
Milch	milk
Milchmixgetränk	milk shake
Milchreis	rice pudding
Mineralwasser	(sparkling) mineral water
Mohnkuchen	poppyseed cake
Möhren	carrots
Mohrrüben	carrots
Most	fruit wine
Mus	purée
Muscheln	mussels
Muskat(nuß)	nutmeg
MWSt = Mehrwertsteuer	VAT

nach Art des Hauses	à la maison
nach Hausfrauenart	home-made
Nachspeisen	desserts
Nachtisch	dessert
Napfkuchen	ring-shaped poundcake
natürlich	natural
Nieren	kidneys
Nudeln	pasta
Nudelsalat	noodle salad
Nudelsuppe	noodle soup
Nüsse	nuts
Obstsalat	fruit salad
Ochsenschwanzsuppe	oxtail soup
Öl	oil
Oliven	olives
Olivenöl	olive oil
Omelett	omelette
Orangen	oranges
Orangensaft	orange juice
Palatschinken	stuffed pancakes
paniert	with breadcrumbs
Paprika	peppers
Paprikasalat	pepper salad
Paprikaschoten	peppers
Paradeiser	tomatoes
Parmesankäse	parmesan cheese
Pastete	vol-au-vent
Pellkartoffeln	potatoes boiled in their jackets
Petersilie	parsley
Petersilienkartoffeln	potatoes with parsley
Pfannkuchen	pancake(s)
Pfeffer	pepper
Pfifferlinge	chanterelles
Pfirsiche	peaches
Pflaumen	plums
Pflaumenkuchen	plum tart
Pflaumenmus	plum jam
Pichelsteiner Topf	vegetable stew with diced beef
pikant	spicy
Pikkolo	quarter bottle of champagne
Pilze	mushrooms

73

Pilzsoße	mushroom sauce
Pilzsuppe	mushroom soup
Platte	selection
pochiert	poached
Pökelfleisch	salt meat
Pommes frites	French fried potatoes
Porree	leek
Potthast	braised beef with sauce
Poularde	young chicken
Preiselbeeren	cranberries
Preßkopf	brawn
Prinzeßbohnen	unsliced runner beans
Pumpernickel	black rye bread
Püree	(potato) purée
püriert	puréed
Putenschenkel	turkey leg
Puter	turkey
Quark	curd cheese
Quarkspeise	curd cheese dish
Radieschen	radishes
Rahm	(sour) cream
Räucheraal	smoked eel
Räucherhering	kipper, smoked herring
Räucherlachs	smoked salmon
Räucherspeck	smoked bacon
Rauchfleisch	smoked meat
Rehbraten	roast venison
Rehgulasch	venison goulash
Rehkeule	haunch of venison
Rehrücken	saddle of venison
Reibekuchen	potato waffles
Reis	rice
Reisauflauf	rice pudding
Reisbrei	creamed rice
Reisrand	with rice
Reissalat	rice salad
Remoulade	remoulade - mayonnaise flavoured with herbs, mustard and capers
Renke	whitefish
Rettich	radish
Rhabarber	rhubarb

Rheinischer Sauerbraten	braised beef
Rinderbraten	pot roast
Rinderfilet	fillet steak
Rinderrouladen	stuffed beef rolls
Rinderzunge	ox tongue
Rindfleisch	beef
Rindfleischsalat	beef salad
Rindfleischsuppe	beef broth
Rippchen	spare ribs
Risi-Pisi	rice and peas
Risotto	risotto
roh	raw
Rohkostplatte	selection of salads
Rollmops	rolled-up pickled herring, rollmops
rosa	rare to medium
Rosenkohl	Brussels sprouts
Rosinen	raisins
Rostbraten	roast
Rostbratwurst	barbecued sausage
Rösti	fried potatoes and onions
Röstkartoffeln	fried potatoes
Rotbarsch	type of perch
Rote Bete	beetroot
rote Grütze	red fruit jelly
Rotkohl	red cabbage
Rotkraut	red cabbage
Rotwein	red wine
Rührei mit Speck	scrambled egg with bacon
Rühreier	scrambled eggs
Rumpsteak	rump steak
Russische Eier	egg mayonnaise
Sahne	cream
Sahnesoße	cream sauce
Sahnetorte	cream gâteau
Salate	salads
Salatplatte	selection of salads
Salatsoße	salad dressing
Salz	salt
Salzburger Nockerln	sweet soufflés
Salzheringe	salted herrings
Salzkartoffeln	boiled potatoes

Salzkruste	salty crusted skin
Sandkuchen	type of Madeira cake
sauer	sour
Sauerbraten	marinaded pot roast
Sauerkraut	white cabbage, finely chopped and pickled
Sauerrahm	sour cream
Schaschlik	(shish-)kebab
Schattenmorellen	morello cherries
Schellfisch	haddock
Schildkrötensuppe	real turtle soup
Schillerlocken	smoked haddock rolls
Schinken	ham
Schinkenröllchen	rolled ham
Schinkenwurst	ham sausage
Schlachtplatte	selection of fresh sausages
Schlagsahne	whipped cream
Schlei	tench
Schmorbraten	pot roast
Schnecken	snails
Schnittlauch	chives
Schnitzel	cutlet
Schokolade	chocolate
Scholle	plaice
Schulterstück	slice of shoulder
Schwarzbrot	brown rye bread
Schwarzwälder Kirschtorte	Black Forest cherry gâteau
Schwarzwurzeln	salsifies
Schweinebauch	belly of pork
Schweinebraten	roast pork
Schweinefilet	fillet of pork
Schweinefleisch	pork
Schweinekotelett	pork chop
Schweineleber	pig's liver
Schweinerippe	cured pork chop
Schweinerollbraten	rolled roast of pork
Schweineschmorbraten	roast pork
Schweineschnitzel	pork fillet
Schweinshaxe	knuckle of pork
Seelachs	pollack *(fish)*
Seezunge	sole

Sekt	sparkling wine, champagne
Sellerie	celery
Selleriesalat	celery salad
Semmel	bread roll
Semmelknödel	bread dumplings
Senf	mustard
Senfsahnesoße	mustard and cream sauce
Senfsoße	mustard sauce
Serbisches Reisfleisch	diced pork, onions, tomatoes and rice
Soleier	pickled eggs
Soße	sauce, gravy
Soufflé	soufflé
Spanferkel	sucking pig
Spargel	asparagus
Spargelcremesuppe	cream of asparagus soup
Spätzle	home-made noodles
Speck	bacon
Speckknödel	bacon dumplings
Specksoße	bacon sauce
Speisekarte	menu
Spezialität des Hauses	speciality
Spiegeleier	fried eggs
Spießbraten	joint roasted on a spit
Spinat	spinach
Spitzkohl	white cabbage
Sprotten	sprats
Sprudel(wasser)	mineral water
Stachelbeeren	gooseberries
Stangen(weiß)brot	French bread
Steak	steak
Steinbutt	turbot
Steinpilze	type of mushroom
Stollen	type of fruit loaf
Strammer Max	ham and fried egg on bread
Streuselkuchen	sponge cake with crumble topping
Sülze	brawn
Suppen	soups
Suppengrün	mixed herbs and vegetables *(used in soup)*
süß	sweet

süß-sauer	sweet-and-sour
Süßspeisen	sweet dishes
Süßwasserfische	freshwater fish
Szegediner Gulasch	goulash with pickled cabbage
Tafelwasser	(still) mineral water
Tafelwein	table wine
Tagesgericht	dish of the day
Tageskarte	menu of the day
Tagessuppe	soup of the day
Tatar	steak tartare
Taube	pigeon
Tee	tea
Teigmantel	pastry case
Thunfisch	tuna
Tintenfisch	squid
Tomaten	tomatoes
Tomatensalat	tomato salad
Tomatensuppe	tomato soup
Törtchen	tart(s)
Torte	gâteau
Truthahn	turkey
überbacken	au gratin
Ungarischer Gulasch	Hungarian goulash
ungebraten	unfried
Vanille	vanilla
Vanillesoße	vanilla sauce
verlorene Eier	poached eggs
Vollkornbrot	dark rye bread
vom Grill	grilled
vom Kalb	veal
vom Rind	beef
vom Rost	grilled
vom Schwein	pork
Vorspeisen	hors d'oeuvres, starters
Waffeln	waffles
Waldorfsalat	salad with celery, apples and walnuts
Wasser	water
Wassermelone	water melon
Weichkäse	soft cheese
Weinbergschnecken	snails

Weinbrand	brandy
Weincreme	pudding with wine
Weinschaumcreme	creamed pudding with wine
Weinsoße	wine sauce
Weintrauben	grapes
Weißbier	fizzy light-coloured beer made with wheat
Weißbrot	white bread
Weißkohl	white cabbage
Weißkraut	white cabbage
Weißwein	white wine
Weißwurst	veal sausage
Weizenbier	fizzy light-coloured beer made with wheat
Wiener Schnitzel	veal in breadcrumbs
Wild	game
Wildschweinkeule	haunch of wild boar
Wildschweinsteak	wild boar steak
Windbeutel	cream puff
Wirsing	savoy cabbage
Wurst	sausage
Würstchen	frankfurter(s)
Wurstplatte	selection of sausages
Wurstsalat	sausage salad
Wurstsülze	sausage brawn
würzig	spicy
Zander	pike-perch, zander
Zigeunerschnitzel	veal with peppers and relishes
Zitrone	lemon
Zitronencreme	lemon cream
Zucchini	courgettes, zucchinis
Zucker	sugar
Zuckererbsen	mange-tout peas
Zunge	tongue
Zungenragout	tongue ragoût
Zutaten	ingredients
Zwiebeln	onions
Zwiebelringe	onion rings
Zwiebelsuppe	onion soup
Zwiebeltorte	onion tart
Zwischengerichte	entrées

SHOPS AND SERVICES

This chapter covers all sorts of shopping needs and services, and to start with you'll find some general phrases which can be used in lots of different places – many of which are named in the list below. After the general phrases come some more specific requests and sentences to use when you've found what you need, be it food, clothing, repairs, film-developing, or a haircut. Don't forget to refer to the mini-dictionary for items you may be looking for.

Shops in Germany are generally open from 9 am to 6.30 pm with some department stores and supermarkets staying open until 8.30 pm on Thursdays. On Saturdays shops normally close at 2 pm, except for the first Saturday of each month, when most remain open until 6 pm.

Hairdressers are generally closed on Mondays.

USEFUL WORDS AND PHRASES

antique shop	der Antiquitäten-laden	*antikvitayten-lahden*
audio equipment	die Phonoartikel	*fono-arteekel*
baker's	der Bäcker	*becker*
boutique	die Boutique	*'boutique'*
butcher's	der Metzger, der Fleischer	*metsger, flysher*
bookshop	die Buchhandlung	*bOOKHhantloong*
buy	kaufen	*kowfen*
cake shop	die Konditorei	*konditor-ry*
camera shop	der Fotoladen	*fotolahden*
camping equipment	die Campingartikel	*kempingarteekel*
carrier bag	die (Trage)tasche	*(trahguh-)tashuh*
cheap	billig	*billish*
china	das Porzellan	*portsellahn*
confectioner's	der Süßwarenladen	*swssvaren-lahden*

cost	kosten	*ko̱sten*
craft shop	der Handwerksladen	*ha̱ntvairks-lahden*
department store	das Kaufhaus	*ko̱wfhowss*
dry cleaner's	die chemische Reinigung	*sha̱ymishuh ry̱nigoong*
electrical goods store	der Elektroladen	*ele̱ktrolahden*
expensive	teuer	*to̱yer*
fishmonger's	das Fischgeschäft	*fi̱sh-gusheft*
florist's	das Blumengeschäft	*blOO̱men-gusheft*
food store	das Lebensmittel-geschäft	*la̱ybensmittel-gusheft*
fruit	das Obst	*ohpst*
gift shop	der Geschenkladen	*gushe̱nk-lahden*
greengrocer's	die Gemüsehandlung	*gumo̱̱zuh-hantloong*
grocer's	das Lebensmittel-geschäft	*la̱ybensmittel-gusheft*
hairdresser's	der Friseur	*frizu̱r*
hardware shop	das Haushaltswaren-geschäft	*ho̱wss-halts-varen-gusheft*
(for DIY etc)	die Eisenwaren-handlung	*i̱ze-en-varen-hantloong*
hypermarket	der Großmarkt	*gro̱hssmarkt*
jeweller's	der Juwelierladen	*yOOvele̱er-lahden*
ladies' wear	die Damen-bekleidung	*da̱hmen-buklydoong*
launderette	der Waschsalon	*va̱sh-salong*
market	der Markt	*ma̱rkt*
menswear	die Herrenbekleidung	*ha̱irren-buklydoong*
newsagent's	der Zeitungsladen	*tsy̱toongs-lahden*
optician's	der Optiker	*o̱ptiker*
receipt	die Quittung	*kvi̱ttoong*
record shop	das Schallplatten-geschäft	*sha̱llplatten-gusheft*
sale	der Schlußverkauf	*shlo̱oss-fairkowf*
shoe repairer's	der Schuhmacher	*shOO̱maKHer*

shoe shop	das Schuhgeschäft	*sh00-gusheft*
shop	der Laden,	*lahden,*
	das Geschäft	*gusheft*
souvenir shop	der Souvenirladen	*z00veneerlahden*
sports equipment	die Sportartikel	*shportarteekel*
sportswear	die Sportkleidung	*shport-klydoong*
stationer's	die Schreibwaren-	*shryp-varen-*
	handlung	*hantloong*
supermarket	der Supermarkt	*z00permarkt*
tailor	der Schneider	*shnyder*
till	die Kasse	*kassuh*
tobacconist's	der Tabakwarenladen	*tabakvaren-lahden*
toyshop	die Spielwaren-	*shpeelvaren-*
	handlung	*hantloong*
travel agent's	das Reisebüro	*ryzuhbüro*
vegetables	das Gemüse	*gumüzuh*
wine merchant's	die Weinhandlung	*vine-hantloong*

Excuse me, where is/are ...? *(in a supermarket)*
Entschuldigung, wo finde ich ...?
ent-shooldigoong vo finduh ish

Where is there a ... (shop)?
Wo gibt es ein Geschäft für ...?
vo geept ess ine gusheft für

Where is the ... department?
Wo ist die ...-Abteilung?
vo ist dee ...-aptyloong

Where is the main shopping area?
Wo ist das Einkaufsviertel?
vo ist dass ine-kowfs-feertel

Is there a market here?
Gibt es hier einen Markt?
geept ess heer ine-en markt

I'd like ...
Ich hätte gern ...
ish hettuh gairn

Do you have ...?
Haben Sie ...?
hahben zee

How much is this?
Was kostet das?
vass kostet dass

Where do I pay?
Wo ist die Kasse?
vo ist dee kassuh

Do you take credit cards?
Akzeptieren Sie Kreditkarten?
aktsepteeren zee kredeetkarten

I think perhaps you've short-changed me
Könnte es sein, daß Sie mir zuwenig herausgegeben haben?
kurntuh ess zine dass zee meer tsOOvaynish hairowss-gugayben hahben

Can I have a receipt?
Kann ich eine Quittung bekommen?
kan ish ine-uh kvittoong bukommen

Can I have a bag, please?
Haben Sie eine Tragetasche, bitte?
hahben zee ine-uh trahguh-tashuh bittuh

I'm just looking
Ich sehe mich nur um
ish zay-uh mish nOOr oom

I'll come back later
Ich komme später wieder
ish kommuh shpayter veeder

Do you have any more of these?
Haben Sie noch mehr hiervon?
hahben zee noKH mair heerfon

Have you anything cheaper?
Haben Sie etwas Billigeres?
hahben zee etvass billigeress

Have you anything larger/smaller?
Haben Sie etwas Größeres/Kleineres?
hahben zee etvass grursseress/kline-eress

Can I try it/them on?
Kann ich es/sie anprobieren?
kan ish ess/zee anprobeeren

Does it come in other colours?
Gibt es das auch in anderen Farben?
geept es dass owKH in anderen farben

Could you gift-wrap it for me?
Könnten Sie es mir als Geschenk einpacken?
kurnten zee ess meer alss gushenk ine-packen

I'd like to exchange this, it's faulty
Ich möchte dies umtauschen, es ist defekt
ish murshtuh deess oomtowshen ess ist dayfekt

I'm afraid I don't have the receipt
Ich habe leider die Quittung nicht
ish hahbuh lyder dee kvittoong nisht

Can I have a refund?
Kann ich mein Geld zurückbekommen?
kan ish mine gelt tsoorwk-bukommen

My camera isn't working
Meine Kamera funktioniert nicht
mine-uh kamera foonkts-yoneert nisht

I want a 36-exposure colour film, 100ISO
Ich hätte gern einen Farbfilm für 36 Aufnahmen, 100ISO
ish hettuh gairn ine-en farpfilm für zex-oont-dryssish owfnahmen,
    hoondert ee-ess-oh

I'd like this film processed
Ich möchte diesen Film entwickeln lassen
ish murshtuh deezen film entvickeln lassen

Matt/glossy prints
Abzüge in matt/Hochglanz
aptsmguh in mat/hohKHglants

One-hour service, please
Ein-Stunden-Service, bitte
ine-shtoonden-'service' bittuh

Where can I get this mended?
Wo kann ich das reparieren lassen?
vo kan ish dass repareeren lassen

(clothes)
Wo kann ich das ausbessern lassen?
vo kan ish dass owssbessern lassen

Can you mend this?
Können Sie das reparieren?
kurnen zee dass repareeren?

(clothes)
Können Sie das ausbessern?
kurnen zee dass owssbessern

I'd like this skirt/these trousers dry-cleaned
Ich möchte diesen Rock/diese Hose chemisch reinigen lassen
ish murshtuh deezen rok/deezuh hohzuh shaymish rynigen lassen

When will it/will they be ready?
Wann ist es/sind sie fertig?
van ist ess/zint zee fairtish

I'd like some change for the washing machine/tumble dryer
Ich hätte gern Kleingeld für die Waschmaschine/den Trockner
ish hettuh gairn kline-gelt fur dee vash-masheenuh/dayn trockner

Can you help me work the machine, please
Können Sie mir helfen, die Maschine zu bedienen?
kurnen zee meer helfen dee masheenuh tsoo budeenen

I'd like to make an appointment
Ich hätte gern einen Termin
ish hettuh gairn ine-en tairmeen

I want a cut and blow-dry
Schneiden und fönen, bitte
shnyden oont furnen bittuh

With conditioner
Mit Pflegespülung
mit pflayguh-shpuloong

No conditioner, thanks
Keine Pflegespülung, danke
kine-uh pflayguh-shpuloong dankuh

Just a trim, please
Nur etwas nachschneiden, bitte
nOOr etvass nahKH-shnyden bittuh

A bit more off here, please
Hier bitte etwas kürzer
heer bittuh etvass kurtser

Not too much off!
Nicht zu kurz!
nisht tsOO koorts

When does the market open?
Wann öffnet der Markt?
van urfnet dair markt

Is there one today in a town nearby?
Gibt es heute einen in einer Stadt in der Nähe?
geept ess hoytuh ine-en in ine-er shtat in dair nay-uh

What's the price per kilo?
Was kostet es pro Kilo?
vass kostet ess pro keelo

Could you write that down please?
Könnten Sie mir das bitte aufschreiben?
kurnten zee meer dass bittuh owfshryben

That's very expensive!
Das ist aber sehr teuer!
dass ist ahber zair toyer

That's fine. I'll take it
In Ordnung. Ich nehme es
in ortnoong ish naymuh ess

I'll have a piece of that cheese
Ich hätte gern ein Stück von dem Käse
ish hettuh gairn ine shtwk fon daym kayzuh

About 250/500 grams
Etwa 250/500 Gramm
etva tsvy-hoondert-fwnftsish/fwnf-hoondert gram

A kilo/half a kilo of apples, please
Ein Kilo/Pfund Äpfel, bitte
ine keelo/pfoont epfel bittuh

A quarter of a kilo of ham, please
Ein halbes Pfund Schinken, bitte
ine halbess pfoont shinken bittuh

May I taste it?
Kann ich einmal probieren?
kan ish ine-mal probeeren

No, I don't like the taste
Nein, das schmeckt mir nicht so gut
nine dass shmekt meer nisht zo gOOt

That's very nice, I'll take some
Das ist sehr lecker, davon nehme ich etwas
dass ist zair lecker dahfon naymuh ish etvass

It isn't what I wanted
Es ist nicht das, was ich wollte
ess ist nisht dass vass ish volltuh

THINGS YOU'LL SEE

Abteilung	department
Ausverkauf	sale
ausverkauft	sold out
Bäckerei	bakery
Blumen	flowers
Buchhandlung	bookshop
Büroartikel	office supplies
chemische Reinigung	dry cleaner's
Coiffeur	hair stylist
Damenkleidung	ladies' clothing
Damensalon	ladies' salon
Drogerie	drugstore, chemist's
Fleischerei	butcher's
Friseur	barber's
Haarstudio	hairdressing studio
Heimwerkerbedarf	DIY supplies
herabgesetzt	reduced
Herrenkleidung	menswear
Herrensalon	men's hairdresser
Kasse	cash point
Kaufhaus	department store

→

Konditorei	cake shop
Lebensmittel	groceries
Metzgerei	butcher's
Mode	fashion
nicht berühren	do not touch
Obergeschoß	upper floor
Obst und Gemüse	fruit and vegetables
Pelze	furs
Preis	price
preiswert	bargain price, inexpensive
reduziert	reduced
Reisebüro	travel agent's
Schreibwaren	stationery
Schuhe	shoes
Schuhreparaturen	shoe repairs, heelbar
Selbstbedienung	self-service
Sommerschlußverkauf	summer sale
Sonderangebot	special offer
Sonderpreis	special price
Spielwaren	toys
Spirituosen	spirits
Spitzenqualität	high quality
Süßwaren	confectionery
Tabakwaren	tobacconist's
täglich frisch	fresh every day
Teppiche	carpets
Tiefgeschoß	lower floor, basement
Umtausch nur gegen Quittung	goods may not be exchanged without a receipt
vergriffen	unavailable, out of stock
vom Umtausch ausgeschlossen	may not be exchanged
Waschsalon	launderette
Winterschlußverkauf	winter sale
Zeitschriften	magazines
Zeitungen	newspapers

THINGS YOU'LL HEAR

Werden Sie schon bedient?
Are you being served?

Kann ich Ihnen helfen?
Can I help you?

Haben Sie es etwas kleiner?
Have you anything smaller? *(money)*

Das haben wir gerade nicht vorrätig
I'm sorry we're out of stock

Das ist alles, was wir haben
This is all we have

Darf es sonst noch etwas sein?
Will there be anything else?

Darf es etwas mehr sein?
Is it okay if it's a bit over?

Wieviel hätten Sie gern?
How much would you like?

Wie möchten Sie es gern?
How would you like it?

Bezahlung mit Kreditkarte ist leider nicht möglich
I'm afraid it's not possible to pay by credit card

SPORT

Whatever your sport and wherever you are in Germany you will find no lack of facilities. The many lakes and rivers, as well as the North Sea and the Baltic Sea coasts, provide excellent opportunities for swimming, sailing, canoeing, fishing (permit required), sailboarding etc, while an extensive network of well-marked footpaths makes Germany an ideal country for walking. Cycling too is popular, and bikes can be hired almost everywhere, including at a large number of railway stations.

Germany is known throughout the world as a centre for winter sports with around 300 resorts, mainly concentrated in the Alps, Black Forest and Harz. In addition, many other areas have good facilities for cross-country skiing, while most of the larger towns have an ice-rink, often open all year round.

USEFUL WORDS AND PHRASES

Alps	die Alpen	_alpen_
athletics	Leichtathletik	_lysht-atlaytik_
badminton	Badminton	_'badminton'_
ball	der Ball	_bal_
bicycle	das Fahrrad	_far-raht_
binding _(ski)_	die Bindung	_bindoong_
canoe	das Kanu	_kahnOO_
canoeing	Kanufahren	_kahnOOfaren_
cross-country skiing	Langlauf	_langlowf_
current	die Strömung	_shtrurmoong_
cycle path	der Radweg	_rahtvayk_
cycling	Radfahren	_rahtfaren_
dive	tauchen	_towKHen_
diving board	das Sprungbrett	_shproongbret_
downhill skiing	Abfahrtslauf	_apfartslowf_
fishing	Angeln	_ang-eln_
fishing rod	die Angelrute	_ang-el-rOOtuh_

flippers	die Schwimmflossen	*shvimflossen*
football	Fußball	*fOOsbal*
football match	das Fußballspiel	*fOOsbal-shpeel*
game	das Spiel	*shpeel*
goggles	die Taucherbrille	*towKHerbrilluh*
golf	Golf	*golf*
golf course	der Golfplatz	*golfplats*
gymnastics	Gymnastik	*gœmnastik*
hang-gliding	Drachenfliegen	*draKHenfleegen*
hillwalking	Bergwandern	*bairkvandern*
hockey	Hockey	*'hockey'*
hunting	die Jagd	*yahkt*
ice-hockey	Eishockey	*ice-'hockey'*
jogging	Jogging	*'jogging'*
mast	der Mast	*mast*
mountaineering	Bergsteigen	*bairk-shtygen*
nursery slope	der Idiotenhügel	*idee-ohten-hœgel*
oars	die Ruder	*rOOder*
oxygen bottle	die Sauerstoffflasche	*zowershtoff-flashuh*
pedal boat	das Tretboot	*traytboht*
piste	die Piste	*pistuh*
racket	der Schläger	*shlayger*
ride	reiten	*rite-en*
riding	Reiten	*rite-en*
riding hat	die Reitermütze	*rite-er-mœtsuh*
rock climbing	Felsenklettern	*felzen-klettern*
row	rudern	*rOOdern*
rowing boat	das Ruderboot	*rOOderboht*
run	laufen	*lowfen*
saddle	der Sattel	*zattel*
sail *(noun)*	das Segel	*zaygel*
(verb)	segeln	*zaygeln*
sailboard	das Windsurfbrett	*vintsurf-bret*
sailing	Segeln	*zaygeln*
go sailing	segeln gehen	*zaygeln gayen*
skate	eislaufen	*ice-lowfen*
skates	die Schlittschuhe	*shlitt-shOO-uh*

skating rink	die Eislaufbahn	*ice-lowfbahn*
ski *(noun)*	der Ski	*shee*
(verb)	Ski fahren	*shee faren*
ski boots	die Skistiefel	*shee-shteefel*
skin diving	Sporttauchen	*shport-towKHen*
skiing	Skilaufen	*sheelowfen*
skilift	der Skilift	*sheelift*
ski pass	der Skipaß	*sheepas*
skisticks	die Skistöcke	*shee-shturkuh*
ski-tow	der Schlepplift	*shlep-lift*
ski trail	die Piste	*pistuh*
ski wax	das Skiwachs	*sheevax*
slalom	der Slalom	*slahlom*
sledge	der Schlitten	*shlitten*
snorkel	der Schnorchel	*shnorshel*
sports centre	das Sportzentrum	*shport-tsentroom*
stadium	das Stadion	*shtahdee-on*
surfboard	das Surfbrett	*surfbrett*
swim	schwimmen	*shvimmen*
swimming costume	der Badeanzug	*bahduh-antsOOk*
swimming pool	das Schwimmbad	*shvimbaht*
team	das Team	*'team'*
tennis	Tennis	*tennis*
tennis court	der Tennisplatz	*tennisplats*
tennis racket	der Tennisschläger	*tennis-shlayger*
toboggan	der Rodelschlitten	*rohdel-shlitten*
volleyball	Volleyball	*vollibal*
walk	wandern	*vandern*
walking	Wandern	*vandern*
water-skiing	Wasserski	*vasser-shee*
water-ski	Wasserski fahren	*vasser-shee faren*
water-skis	die Wasserskier	*vasser-shee-er*
wet suit	der Tauchanzug	*towKHantsOOk*
go windsurfing	windsurfen gehen	*vintsurfen gayen*
winter sports	der Wintersport	*vintershport*
yacht	die Jacht	*yaKHt*

How do I get to the beach?
Wie komme ich zum Strand?
vee kommuh ish tsoom shtrant

How deep is the water here?
Wie tief ist das Wasser hier?
vee teef ist dass vasser heer

Is there an indoor/outdoor pool here?
Gibt es hier ein Hallenbad/Freibad?
geept ess heer ine hal-en-baht/frybaht

Is it safe to swim here?
Ist das Schwimmen hier ungefährlich?
ist dass shvimmen heer oongefairlish

Can I fish here?
Kann man hier angeln?
kan man heer ang-eln

Do I need a licence?
Braucht man eine Genehmigung?
browKHt man ine-uh gunaymigoong

Is there a golf course near here?
Gibt es in der Nähe einen Golfplatz?
geept ess in dair nay-uh ine-en golfplats

Do I have to be a member?
Muß man Mitglied sein?
mooss man mitgleet zine

I would like to hire a bicycle/some skis
Ich möchte ein Fahrrad/Skier leihen
ish murshtuh ine far-raht/shee-er ly-en

How much does it cost per hour/day?
Was kostet es pro Stunde/Tag?
vass kostet ess pro shtoonduh/tahk

I would like to take water-skiing lessons
Ich möchte gern Wasserskiunterricht nehmen
ish murshtuh gairn vasserskee-oonterrisht naymen

Where can I hire ...?
Wo kann man ... leihen?
vo kan man ... ly-en

There's something wrong with this binding
Mit dieser Bindung stimmt etwas nicht
mit deezer bindoong shtimmt etvass nisht

How much is a weekly pass for the skilift?
Was kostet ein Wochenpaß für den Skilift?
vass kostet ine voKHen-pas fur dayn sheelift

What are the snow conditions like today?
Wie sind heute die Schneeverhältnisse?
vee zint hoytuh dee shnay-fairheltnissuh

I'd like to try cross-country skiing
Ich möchte gern Langlauf probieren
ish murshtuh gairn langlowf probeeren

I haven't played this before
Das habe ich noch nie gespielt
das hahbuh ish noKH nee gushpeelt

Let's go skating/swimming
Sollen wir eislaufen/schwimmen gehen?
zollen veer ice-lowfen/shvimmen gayen

What's the score?
Wie steht's?
vee shtayts

Who won?
Wer hat gewonnen?
vair hat guvonnen

THINGS YOU'LL SEE

Angeln verboten	no fishing
Betreten der Eisfläche verboten	keep off the ice
Bootsverleih	boat hire
Eisstadion	ice rink
Fahrräder	bicycles
Fahrradverleih	bicycles for hire
Fahrradweg	cycle path
Freibad	open-air swimming pool
Gefahr	danger
gefährliche Strömung	dangerous current
Hafen	port
Hafenpolizei	harbour police
Hallenbad	indoor swimming pool
Karten	tickets
Lawinengefahr	danger of avalanches
Radweg	cycle path
Reitweg	bridle path
Rodelbahn	toboggan run
Schneeverwehung	snow drift
Schwimmen verboten	no swimming
Segelboote	sailing boats
Skipiste	ski slope
Sportzentrum	sports centre
Sprungschanze	ski jump
Stadion	stadium
Strand	beach
Tauchen verboten	no diving
Tauwetter	thaw
Umkleidekabine	changing rooms
Wanderweg	trail
Wassersport	water sports
zum Skilift	to the skilift
zu verleihen	for hire

POST OFFICES AND BANKS

Post offices can be identified by a yellow sign with the word
Post(amt) or the symbol of a post horn. Opening hours are
usually from 9 am to 11.30 am and from 2 pm to 5.30 pm on
Monday to Friday with a 9 till 12 noon Saturday opening.
Postboxes are yellow.

Most banks are open from 8.30 am or 9 am to 12.30 pm and
from 1.30 pm to 4 pm. On Thursdays they stay open until 6 pm.
Banks are closed on Saturdays and Sundays. Foreign currency
and traveller's cheques can also be exchanged at some of the larger
hotels or at a bureau de change (**Wechselstube**). When changing
money in a bank, it is customary to make your transaction at one
desk and then go to a different desk, the cash desk or **Kasse**, where
your money will be paid out to you.

The German unit of currency is the **Mark**. One **Mark** is divided
into 100 **Pfennige**. Coins come in denominations of 1, 2, 5, 10
and 50 Pfennige, 1 Mark, 2 and 5 Marks. Notes are available in 10,
20, 50, 100, 200, 500 and 1,000 denominations.

Credit cards are not that widely used in Germany, so don't be
surprised if a shop or a railway station declines to accept payment
by credit card.

USEFUL WORDS AND PHRASES

airmail	Luftpost	*looftposst*
bank	die Bank	*bank*
banknote	der Geldschein	*gelt-shine*
cash	das Bargeld	*bargelt*
cash dispenser	der Geldautomat	*gelt-owtomaht*
change	wechseln	*vexeln*
cheque	der Scheck	*shek*
cheque book	das Scheckbuch	*shekbOOKH*
collection	die Leerung	*layroong*
counter	der Schalter	*shalter*
credit card	die Kreditkarte	*kredeet-kartuh*

customs form	das Zollformular	*tsoll-formOOlar*
delivery	die Zustellung	*tsOO-shtelloong*
deposit *(noun)*	die Einzahlung	*ine-tsahloong*
(verb)	einzahlen	*ine-tsahlen*
exchange rate	der Wechselkurs	*vexel-koors*
fax *(noun)*	das Fax	*fax*
(verb: document)	faxen	*faxen*
form	das Formular	*formOOlar*
international	die Auslands-	*owss-lants-*
money order	postanweisung	*posst-anvyzoong*
letter	der Brief	*breef*
letter box	der Briefkasten	*breefkasten*
mail	die Post	*posst*
money order	die Postanweisung	*posst-anvyzoong*
package/parcel	das Paket	*pakayt*
post	die Post	*posst*
postage rates	das Porto	*porto*
postal order	die Geldanweisung	*gelt-anvyzoong*
postcard	die Ansichtskarte	*anzishts-kartuh*
postcode	die Postleitzahl	*posstlite-tsahl*
poste-restante	postlagernde	*posst-lahgernduh*
	Sendungen	*zendoong-en*
postman	der Briefträger	*breef-trayger*
post office	das Postamt	*posst-amt*
pound sterling	das englische Pfund	*eng-lishuh pfoont*
registered	das Einschreiben	*ine-shryben*
letter		
stamp	die Briefmarke	*breef-markuh*
surface mail	Post auf dem	*posst owf daym*
	Landweg	*lantvayk*
telegram	das Telegramm	*telegram*
traveller's	der Reisescheck	*ryzuh-shek*
cheque		
withdraw	abheben	*ap-hayben*
withdrawal	die Abhebung	*ap-hayboong*

How much is a letter/postcard to England?
Was ist das Porto für einen Brief/eine Postkarte nach England?
vass ist dass porto fur ine-en breef/ine-uh posstkartuh nahKH englant

I would like three 1 mark stamps
Ich hätte gern drei Briefmarken zu einer Mark
ish hettuh gairn dry breef-marken tsoo ine-er mark

I want to register this letter
Ich möchte diesen Brief als Einschreiben senden
ish murshtuh deezen breef alss ine-shryben zenden

I want to send this parcel to Scotland
Ich möchte dieses Paket nach Schottland senden
ish murshtuh deezes pakayt nahKH shotlant zenden

How long does the post to America take?
Wie lange ist die Post nach Amerika unterwegs?
vee languh ist dee posst nahKH amayrika oontervayks

Where can I post this?
Wo kann ich das aufgeben?
vo kan ish dass owfgayben

Is there any mail for me?
Ist Post für mich da?
ist posst fur mish da

I'd like to send a telegram/fax
Ich möchte ein Telegramm/Fax schicken
ish murshtuh ine telegram/fax shicken

This is to go airmail
Ich möchte dies mit Luftpost senden
ish murshtuh deess mit looftposst zenden

I'd like to change this into marks
Ich möchte dies gern in D-Mark wechseln
ish murshtuh deess gairn in day-mark vexeln

Can I cash these traveller's cheques?
Kann ich diese Reiseschecks einlösen?
kan ish deezuh ryzuh-sheks ine-lurzen

What is the exchange rate for the pound?
Was ist der Wechselkurs für das Pfund?
vass ist dair vexel-koors fɯr dass pfoont

Can I draw cash using this credit card?
Kann ich mit dieser Kreditkarte Geld abheben?
kan ish mit deezer kredeet-kartuh gelt ap-hayben

I'd like it in 50 Mark notes
Ich möchte es gern in 50-Mark-Scheinen
ish murshtuh ess gairn in fɯnftsish-mark-shine-en

Could you give me smaller notes?
Könnten Sie es mir in kleineren Scheinen geben?
kurnten zee ess meer in kline-eren shine-en gayben

THINGS YOU'LL SEE

Absender	sender
ausfüllen	fill in
ausländische Währungen	foreign currency
Auslandsporto	overseas postage
Auszahlungen	withdrawals, cash desk
Brief	letter
Briefmarken	stamps
Bundespost	Federal Post Office
Drucksachen	printed matter
Einschreibsendungen	registered mail
Einzahlungen	deposits
Empfänger	addressee
Gebühren	charges
Geldautomat	cash dispenser

→

Geldwechsel	currency exchange
geöffnet	open
geschlossen	closed
Hausnummer	number
Inlandsporto	inland postage
Kasse	cash desk
Luftpostsendungen	airmail
nächste Leerung	next collection
Öffnungszeiten	opening hours
Ort	town, place
Päckchen	small parcels
Paket	parcels
Paketannahme	parcels counter
Porto	postage
Postamt	post office
Postanweisungen	money orders
Postkarte	postcard
postlagernde Sendungen	poste-restante
Postleitzahl	postcode
Postsparkasse	giro bank
Postwertzeichen in kleinen Mengen	stamps in small quantities
Schalter	counter
Sparkasse	savings bank
Telefonzelle	telephone box
Wechselkurs	exchange rate
Wechselstube	bureau de change

YOU MAY HEAR

Sie bekommen Ihr Geld an der Kasse
You'll get your money at the cash desk

TELEPHONES

Telephone boxes in Germany are yellow. International calls can only be made from boxes that show a green disc with the word **Ausland** or **International.** To telephone the UK, dial 0044 followed by the area code (but omit the 0 which prefixes all UK area codes) and the number you want. To call a number in the USA, dial 001 followed by the area code and subscriber's number. Phonecards can be bought from post offices.

The tones you'll hear when telephoning in Germany are:

Dialling tone:	same as in UK and USA
Ringing:	long high-pitched tone
Engaged:	rapid pips similar to UK and USA
Unobtainable:	voice says 'Kein Anschluß unter dieser Nummer', and you'll hear 3 short pips of ascending pitch.

In German, telephone numbers are read out in pairs of numbers, for example 302106 is said **dreißig, einundzwanzig, null sechs** (thirty, twenty-one, zero six). It will, of course, also be perfectly comprehensible to say a number as individual digits.

USEFUL WORDS AND PHRASES

call *(noun)*	der Anruf	*anrOOf*
(verb)	anrufen	*anrOOfen*
cardphone	das Kartentelefon	*karten-telefohn*
code	die Vorwahl	*forvahl*
crossed line	die Fehlverbindung	*fayl-fairbindoong*
dial	wählen	*vaylen*
dialling tone	das Amtszeichen	*amts-tsyshen*
enquiries	die Auskunft	*owsskoonft*
extension	der Nebenanschluß	*nayben-anshlooss*
international call	das Auslands-gespräch	*owsslants-gushpraysh*
number	die Nummer	*noommer*

operator	die Vermittlung	*fairmittloong*
pay-phone	das Münztelefon	*mœnts-telefohn*
phonecard	die Telefonkarte	*telefohn-kartuh*
receiver	der Hörer	*hur-er*
reverse charge call	das R-Gespräch	*air-gushpraysh*
telephone	das Telefon	*telefohn*
telephone box	die Telefonzelle	*telefohn-tselluh*
telephone directory	das Telefonbuch	*telefohn-bOOKH*
wrong number	die falsche Nummer	*falshuh noommer*

Where is the nearest phone box?
Wo ist die nächste Telefonzelle?
vo ist dee naykstuh telefohn-tselluh

Is there a telephone directory?
Gibt es ein Telefonbuch?
geept ess ine telefohn-bOOKH

I would like the directory for ...
Ich hätte gern das Telefonbuch für ...
ish hettuh gairn dass telefohn-bOOKH fuer

Can I call abroad from here?
Kann man von hier ins Ausland anrufen?
kan man fon heer inss owsslant anrOOfen

I would like to reverse the charges
Ich möchte ein R-Gespräch führen
ish murshtuh ine air-gushpraysh fueren

I would like a number in Wiesbaden
Ich hätte gern eine Nummer in Wiesbaden
ish hettuh gairn ine-uh noommer in veessbahden

Could you give me an outside line?
Geben Sie mir bitte ein Amt
gayben zee meer bittuh ine amt

How do I get an outside line?
Wie kann ich nach draußen telefonieren?
vee kan ish nahKH drowssen telefoneeren

Hello, this is Chris speaking
Hallo, hier spricht Chris
hallo heer shprisht 'Chris'

Is that Monika?
Ist das Monika?
ist dass mohnika

Speaking
Am Apparat
am aparaht

I would like to speak to Angelika
Kann ich bitte Angelika sprechen?
kan ish bittuh angaylika shpreshen

Extension 205 please
Anschluß 205, bitte
anshlooss tsvyhoondertf$\underline{u}$nf bittuh

Please tell him/her Derek called
Bitte sagen Sie ihm/ihr, daß Derek angerufen hat
bittuh zahgen zee eem/eer dass 'Derek' angurOOfen hat

Would you ask him/her to call me back, please
Sagen Sie ihm/ihr bitte, er/sie möchte mich zurückrufen
zahgen zee eem/eer bittuh air/zee murshtuh mish tsoorwk-rOOfen

My number is Cologne 32 14 24
Meine Nummer ist Köln 32 14 24
mine-uh noommer ist kurln tsvy-oont-dr$\underline{y}$sish feertsayn feer-oont-tsvantsish

Do you know where he/she is?
Wissen Sie, wo er/sie ist?
vissen zee vo air/zee ist

When will he/she be back?
Wann wird er/sie zurück sein?
van veert air/zee tsoor m*k zine*

Could you leave him/her a message?
Können Sie ihm/ihr etwas ausrichten?
kurnen zee eem/eer etvass owssrishten

I'll ring back later
Ich rufe später zurück
ish rOOfuh shpayter tsoor m*k*

Sorry, you've got the wrong number
Tut mir leid, Sie sind falsch verbunden
tOOt meer lite zee zint falsh fairboonden

Sorry, (I've got the) wrong number
Tut mir leid, ich habe mich verwählt
tOOt meer lite ish hahbuh mish fairvaylt

THE ALPHABET

a	*ah*	**h**	*hah*	**o**	*o*	**v** *fow*
b	*bay*	**i**	*ee*	**p**	*pay*	**w** *vay*
c	*tsay*	**j**	*yot*	**q**	*kOO*	**x** *ix*
d	*day*	**k**	*kah*	**r**	*air*	**y** *m*psilon
e	*ay*	**l**	*el*	**s**	*ess*	**z** *tset*
f	*ef*	**m**	*em*	**t**	*tay*	
g	*gay*	**n**	*en*	**u**	*OO*	

SPECIAL GERMAN CHARACTERS

ä	*eh*	**ö**	*ur*	**ü**	*m*	**ß** *ess-tset*

THINGS YOU'LL SEE

abnehmen	lift (the receiver)
Apparat	telephone
Auskunft	(directory) enquiries
Auslandsgespräche	international calls
außer Betrieb	out of order
besetzt	engaged
defekt	out of order
Durchwahl	direct dialling
Einheit	unit
fasse dich kurz!	be brief!
Ferngespräche	long-distance calls
Fernsprecher	telephone
Feuer	fire
Feuerwehr	fire brigade
Gabel	hook
Gelbe Seiten	yellow pages
Geld einwerfen	insert money
Gespräch	call, conversation
Großbritannien	Great Britain
Hörer	receiver
Karte ganz einschieben	push card right in
Münzen	coins
Notruf	emergency call
Ortsgespräche	local calls
Rufnummer	number
Störungsstelle	faults service
Telefonzelle	telephone box
Vereinigtes Königreich	United Kingdom
Vermittlung	operator
Vorwahl	code
wählen	to dial
warten	to wait

REPLIES YOU MAY BE GIVEN

Am Apparat
Speaking

Wen möchten Sie sprechen?
Who would you like to speak to?

Sie sind falsch verbunden
You've got the wrong number

Wer spricht bitte?
Who's speaking?

Welche Nummer haben Sie?
What is your number?

Tut mir leid, er ist nicht im Hause
Sorry, he's not here

Er ist um drei Uhr zurück
He'll be back at three o'clock

Bitte rufen Sie morgen nochmal an
Please call again tomorrow

Ich werde ihm/ihr sagen, daß Sie angerufen haben
I'll tell him/her you called

Kein Anschluß unter dieser Nummer
Number unobtainable

Ich verbinde
I'll put you through

Bitte warten
Please hold

EMERGENCIES

In an emergency dial 110 for police or ambulance and 112 for fire. Motorists can get assistance from the **ADAC**, the German motoring organization. If you break down on an autobahn, look for a small arrow on the marker posts at the side of the road: the arrow points in the direction of the nearest emergency telephone. Ask for the **Straßenwacht** *shtrahssen-vaKHt*. Assistance will be free, but you will have to pay for parts.

USEFUL WORDS AND PHRASES

accident	der Unfall	*oonfal*
ambulance	der Krankenwagen	*kranken-vahgen*
assault *(verb)*	überfallen	*ωberfal-en*
breakdown	die Panne	*pannuh*
break down	eine Panne haben	*ine-uh pannuh hahben*
breakdown recovery	der Abschleppdienst	*ap-shlep-deenst*
burglar	der Einbrecher	*ine-breKHer*
burglary	der Einbruch	*ine-brooKH*
casualty department	die Unfallstation	*oonfal-stats-yohn*
crash	der Zusammenstoß	*tsoozammen-shtohss*
emergency	der Notfall	*nohtfal*
fire	das Feuer	*foyer*
fire brigade	die Feuerwehr	*foyer-vayr*
flood	die Überschwem-mung	*ωbershvemmoong*
injured	verletzt	*fairletst*
lose	verlieren	*fairleeren*
pickpocket	der Taschendieb	*tashendeep*
police	die Polizei	*poli-tsy*
police station	die Polizeiwache	*poli-tsy-vaKHuh*
rob	rauben	*rowben*
steal	stehlen	*shtaylen*

108

theft	der Diebstahl	*deep-shtahl*
thief	der Dieb	*deep*
tow	abschleppen	*ap-shleppen*

Help!
Hilfe!
hilfuh

Look out!
Passen Sie auf!
pas-en zee owf

Stop!
Halt!
halt

This is an emergency!
Dies ist ein Notfall!
deess ist ine nohtfal

Get an ambulance!
Rufen Sie einen Krankenwagen!
rOOfen zee ine-en kranken-vahgen

Hurry up!
Beeilen Sie sich!
buh-ile-en zee zish

Please send an ambulance to ...
Bitte schicken Sie einen Krankenwagen zu ...
bittuh shicken zee ine-en kranken-vahgen tsoo

Please come to ...
Bitte kommen Sie zu ...
bittuh kommen zee tsoo

My address is ...
Meine Adresse ist ...
mine-uh adressuh ist

We've had a break-in
Bei uns ist eingebrochen worden
by oonss ist ine-gubroKHen vorden

There's a fire at ...
Es brennt in ...
ess brennt in

Someone's been injured/knocked down
Jemand ist verletzt/niedergeschlagen worden
yaymant ist fairletst/needer-gushlahgen vorden

He's passed out
Er ist ohnmächtig
air ist ohnmeshtish

My passport/car has been stolen
Mein Paß/Auto ist gestohlen worden
mine pas/owto ist gushtohlen vorden

I've lost my traveller's cheques
Ich habe meine Reiseschecks verloren
ish hahbuh mine-uh ryzuh-sheks fairloren

I want to report a stolen credit card
Ich möchte den Diebstahl einer Kreditkarte melden
ish murshtuh dayn deep-shtahl ine-er kredeet-kartuh melden

It was stolen from my room
Es wurde aus meinem Zimmer gestohlen
ess voorduh owss mine-em tsimmer gushtohlen

I lost it in the park/on the train
Ich habe es im Park/im Zug verloren
ish hahbuh ess im park/im tsOOk fairlohren

My luggage has gone missing
Mein Gepäck ist verschwunden
mine gupek ist fairshvoonden

Has my luggage turned up yet?
Ist mein Gepäck schon wieder aufgetaucht?
ist mine gupek shohn veeder owfgutowKHt

The registration number is ...
Mein amtliches Kennzeichen ist ...
mine amtlishes ken-tsyshen ist

My car's been broken into
Mein Auto ist aufgebrochen worden
mine owto ist owfgubroKHen vorden

I've had a crash
Ich habe einen Unfall gehabt
ish hahbuh ine-en oonfal guhahpt

I've been mugged
Ich bin überfallen worden
ish bin ωberfal-en vorden

My son's missing
Mein Sohn ist verschwunden
mine zohn ist fairshvoonden

He has fair/brown hair
Er hat helles/braunes Haar
air hat helless/browness har

He's ... years old
Er ist ... Jahre alt
air ist ... yaruh alt

I've locked myself out
Ich habe mich ausgesperrt
ish hahbuh mish owss-gushpairt

He's drowning
Er ist am Ertrinken
air ist am airtrinken

She can't swim
Sie kann nicht schwimmen
zee kan nisht shvimmen

THINGS YOU'LL SEE

Bergwacht	mountain rescue
Brand	fire
Erste Hilfe	first aid
Feuer	fire
Feuerlöscher	fire extinguisher
Krankenhaus	hospital
Lebensgefahr	danger of death
Nachtdienst	late night chemist *etc*
Notarzt	emergency doctor
Notausgang	emergency exit
Notfälle	emergencies
Notruf	emergency call
Polizei	police
Polizeiwache	police station
Rufsäule	emergency telephone
Unfallrettung	ambulance, emergency service
Unfallstation	casualty department
Verkehrspolizei	traffic police

THINGS YOU'LL HEAR

Wo wohnen Sie?
What's your address?

Wo sind Sie?
Where are you?

Können Sie es/ihn beschreiben?
Can you describe it/him?

HEALTH

Under EC Social Security regulations visitors from the UK qualify for free medical treatment on the same basis as Germans themselves. If you want to make sure of being in possession of all necessary documentation, you should obtain a T4 from a main post office, fill in the attached E111 and get it stamped at the post office before travelling. With the E111, you'll also get a leaflet explaining how to obtain treatment.

In Germany all chemists' shops are independent private concerns. There are no chainstore chemists like Boots in Britain. They sell exclusively medicines and a small assortment of drugstore goods which have some medicinal use. In every town you will find a chemist or **Apotheke** *apotaykuh* that is open all night or over the weekend. Those that are closed will display a notice showing which one is open, and the local newspaper will also advertise the **dienstbereit** *deenstburite* or duty chemist. You may have to ring the night bell.

USEFUL WORDS AND PHRASES

ambulance	der Krankenwagen	*kranken-vahgen*
anaemic	blutarm	*blOOtarm*
appendicitis	die Blinddarm-entzündung	*blintdarm-ent-tsⓤndoong*
aspirin	die Kopfschmerz-tablette	*kopfshmairts-tablettuh*
asthma	das Asthma	*astma*
backache	die Rückenschmerzen	*rⓤken-shmairtsen*
bandage	der Verband	*fairbant*
bite *(by dog)*	der Biß	*biss*
(by insect)	der Stich	*shtish*
bladder	die Blase	*blahzuh*
blister	die Blase	*blahzuh*
blood	das Blut	*blOOt*
blood donor	der Blutspender	*blOOt-shpender*

113

burn	die Verbrennung	*fairbrennoong*
cancer	der Krebs	*krayps*
chemist	die Apotheke	*apotaykuh*
chest	die Brust	*broost*
chickenpox	die Windpocken	*vintpocken*
cold	die Erkältung	*airkeltoong*
concussion	die Gehirn-erschütterung	*guheern-airshwteroong*
constipation	die Verstopfung	*fairshtopfoong*
corn	das Hühnerauge	*hwner-owguh*
cough	der Husten	*hOOsten*
cut	der Schnitt	*shnit*
dentist	der Zahnarzt	*tsahn-artst*
diabetes	die Zuckerkrankheit	*tsooker-krankhite*
diarrhoea	der Durchfall	*doorshfal*
dizzy	schwindlig	*shvintlish*
doctor	der Arzt	*artst*
earache	die Ohrenschmerzen	*oren-shmairtsen*
fever	das Fieber	*feeber*
filling	die Füllung	*fwlloong*
first aid	die Erste Hilfe	*airstuh hilfuh*
flu	die Grippe	*grippuh*
fracture	der Bruch	*brooKH*
German measles	die Röteln	*rurteln*
glasses	die Brille	*brilluh*
haemorrhage	die Blutung	*blOOtoong*
hayfever	der Heuschnupfen	*hoyshnoopfen*
headache	die Kopfschmerzen	*kopf-shmairtsen*
heart	das Herz	*hairts*
heart attack	der Herzinfarkt	*hairts-infarkt*
hospital	das Krankenhaus	*kranken-howss*
ill	krank	*krank*
indigestion	die Magen-verstimmung	*mahgen-fairshtimmoong*
injection	die Spritze	*shpritsuh*
itch	das Jucken	*yoocken*

kidney	die Niere	_neeruh_
lump	der Knoten	_k-nohten_
measles	die Masern	_mahzern_
migraine	die Migräne	_migraynuh_
mumps	der Mumps	_moomps_
nausea	die Übelkeit	_@belkite_
nurse	die Krankenschwester	_kranken-shvester_
(male)	der Krankenpfleger	_kranken-pflayger_
operation	die Operation	_operats-yohn_
pain	der Schmerz	_shmairts_
penicillin	das Penizillin	_penitsileen_
plaster _(sticky)_	das Pflaster	_pflaster_
plaster of Paris	der Gips	_gips_
pneumonia	die Lungen- entzündung	_loongen-ents@ndoong_
pregnant	schwanger	_shvanger_
prescription	das Rezept	_retsept_
rheumatism	das Rheuma	_royma_
scald	die Verbrühung	_fairbr@-oong_
scratch	der Kratzer	_kratser_
smallpox	die Pocken	_pocken_
sore throat	die Halsschmerzen	_halss-shmairtsen_
splinter	der Splitter	_shplitter_
sprain	die Verstauchung	_fairshtowKHoong_
sting	der Stich	_shtish_
stomach	der Magen, der Bauch	_mahgen,_ _bowKH_
temperature	das Fieber	_feeber_
tonsils	die Mandeln	_mandeln_
toothache	die Zahnschmerzen	_tsahn-shmairtsen_
travel sickness	die Reisekrankheit	_ryzuh-krankhite_
ulcer	das Geschwür	_gushv@r_
vaccination	die Impfung	_impfoong_
vomit	erbrechen	_airbreshen_
whooping cough	der Keuchhusten	_koysh-hOOsten_
wound	die Wunde	_voonduh_

I have a pain in …
Ich habe Schmerzen in …
ish hahbuh shmairtsen in

I do not feel well
Ich fühle mich nicht wohl
ish fuuluh mish nisht vohl

I feel sick
Mir ist übel
meer ist uubel

I feel dizzy
Mir ist ganz schwindlig
meer ist gants shvindlish

It hurts here
Es tut hier weh
ess tOOt heer vay

It's a sharp/dull pain
Es ist ein heftiger/dumpfer Schmerz
ess ist ine heftiger/doompfer shmairts

It hurts all the time
Es tut ständig weh
ess tOOt shtendish vay

It only hurts now and then
Es tut nur ab und zu weh
ess tOOt nOOr ap oont tsOO vay

It hurts when you touch it
Es tut weh, wenn man daraufdrückt
ess tOOt vay ven man darowfdrukt

It hurts more at night
Nachts ist es schlimmer
naKHts ist ess shlimmer

116

It stings/it aches/it itches
Es brennt/es tut weh/es juckt
ess brennt/ess tOOt vay/ess yookt

I have a temperature
Ich habe Fieber
ish hahbuh feeber

I need a prescription for ...
Ich brauche ein Rezept für ...
ish browKHuh ine retsept für

I normally take ...
Ich nehme normalerweise ...
ish naymuh normahler-vyzuh

I'm allergic to ...
Ich bin allergisch gegen ...
ish bin alairgish gaygen

Have you got anything for ...?
Haben Sie etwas gegen ...?
hahben zee etvass gaygen

I have lost a filling
Ich habe eine Füllung verloren
ish hahbuh ine-uh fülloong fairloren

Will he/she be all right?
Wird er/sie wieder in Ordnung kommen?
veert air/zee veeder in ortnoong kommen

Will he/she need an operation?
Muß er/sie operiert werden?
mooss air/zee opereert vairden

How is he/she?
Wie geht es ihm/ihr?
vee gayt ess eem/eer

117

THINGS YOU'LL SEE

Ambulanz	out-patients
Arzt	doctor
Augenarzt	ophthalmologist, optician
Augenoptiker	optician
Bereitschaftsdienst	duty doctor/chemist
Blutdruck	blood pressure
dienstbereit	on duty
Erste Hilfe	first aid
Facharzt für ...	specialist for ...
Frauenarzt	gynaecologist
Hals, Nasen, Ohren	ear, nose and throat
Intensivstation	intensive care unit
Krankenhaus	hospital
Krankenkasse	medical insurance
Krankenwagen	ambulance
Medikament	medicine
Notarzt	emergency doctor
Notaufnahme	casualty department
Notfälle	emergencies
Praktischer Arzt	GP
Rezept	prescription
Sanitätsdienst	ambulance service
Sanitätsstelle	first aid centre
Sprechstunde	surgery
Spritze	injection
Untersuchung	check-up
Termin	appointment
Wartezimmer	waiting room
Zahnarzt	dentist

THINGS YOU'LL HEAR

Nehmen Sie jeweils … Tabletten
Take … pills/tablets at a time

Mit Wasser
With water

Zum Zerkauen
Chew them

Einmal/zweimal/dreimal täglich
Once/twice/three times a day

Nur vor dem Schlafengehen
Only when you go to bed

Was nehmen Sie sonst?
What do you normally take?

Sie sollten besser zum Arzt gehen
I think you should see a doctor

Tut mir leid, das haben wir nicht
I'm sorry, we don't have that

Dafür brauchen Sie ein Rezept
For that you need a prescription

Auf nüchternen Magen
On an empty stomach

Der nächste bitte!
Next please!

CONVERSION TABLES

DISTANCES

A mile is 1.6km. To convert kilometres to miles, divide the km by 8 and multiply by 5. Convert miles to km by dividing the miles by 5 and multiplying by 8.

miles	0.62	1.24	1.86	2.43	3.11	3.73	4.35	6.21
miles or km	**1**	**2**	**3**	**4**	**5**	**6**	**7**	**10**
km	1.61	3.22	4.83	6.44	8.05	9.66	11.27	16.10

WEIGHTS

The kilogram is equivalent to 2lb 3oz. To convert kg to lbs, divide by 5 and multiply by 11. One ounce is about 28 grams, and eight ounces about 227 grams; 1lb is therefore about 454 grams.

lbs	2.20	4.41	6.61	8.82	11.02	13.23	19.84	22.04
lbs or kg	**1**	**2**	**3**	**4**	**5**	**6**	**9**	**10**
kg	0.45	0.91	1.36	1.81	2.27	2.72	4.08	4.53

TEMPERATURE

To convert Celsius degrees into Fahrenheit, the accurate method is to multiply the °C figure by 1.8 and add 32. Similarly, to convert °F to °C, subtract 32 from the °F figure and divide by 1.8.

°C	-10	0	5	10	20	30	36.9	40	100
°F	14	32	41	50	68	77	98.4	104	212

LIQUIDS

A litre is about 1.75 pints; a gallon is roughly 4.5 litres.

gals	0.22	0.44	1.10	2.20	4.40	6.60	11.00
gals or litres	**1**	**2**	**5**	**10**	**20**	**30**	**50**
litres	4.54	9.10	22.73	45.46	90.92	136.40	227.30

TYRE PRESSURES

lb/sq in	18	20	22	24	26	28	30	33
kg/sq cm	1.3	1.4	1.5	1.7	1.8	2.0	2.1	2.3

MINI-DICTIONARY

The word for 'the' can be either 'der', 'die' or 'das', depending on whether a noun is masculine, feminine or neuter. The plural is 'die'. The corresponding words for 'a' are 'ein', 'eine' or 'ein'.

a ein, eine
about: about 16 etwa 16
accelerator das Gaspedal
accident der Unfall
accommodation die Unterkunft
ache der Schmerz
adaptor der Adapter
address die Adresse
adhesive der Klebstoff
after nach
aftershave das Rasierwasser
again nochmals
against gegen
agent der Vertreter
Aids Aids
air *(noun)* die Luft
air-conditioning die Klimaanlage
aircraft das Flugzeug
air hostess die Stewardess
airline die Fluglinie
airport der Flughafen
airport bus der Flughafenbus
aisle der Gang
alarm clock der Wecker
alcohol der Alkohol
all alle(s)
  all the streets alle Straßen
  that's all das ist alles
almost fast
alone allein
already schon
always immer
am: I am ich bin
ambulance der Krankenwagen
America Amerika
American *(man)* der Amerikaner

  (woman) die Amerikanerin
  (adj) amerikanisch
and und
ankle der Knöchel
anorak der Anorak
another *(different)* ein anderer
  (one more) noch ein
  another room ein anderes Zimmer
  another coffee, please noch einen Kaffee, bitte
anti-freeze das Frostschutzmittel
antique shop das Antiquitätengeschäft
antiseptic das Antiseptikum
apartment die Wohnung
aperitif der Aperitif
appetite der Appetit
apple der Apfel
application form das Antragsformular
appointment der Termin
apricot die Aprikose
are: we/they are wir/sie sind
  you are Sie sind
  (sing, familiar) du bist
arm der Arm
art die Kunst
art gallery die Kunstgalerie
artist der Künstler
  (female) die Künstlerin
as: as soon as possible so bald wie möglich
ashtray der Aschenbecher
asleep: he's asleep er schläft
aspirin das Kopfschmerztablette

at: at the post office auf der Post
  at the station am Bahnhof
  at night in der Nacht
  at 3 o'clock um 3 Uhr
attractive attraktiv
aunt die Tante
Australia Australien
Australian *(man)* der Australier
  (woman) die Australierin
  (adj) australisch
Austria Österreich
Austrian *(man)* der Österreicher
  (woman) die Österreicherin
  (adj) österreichisch
automatic automatisch
away: is it far away? ist es weit
  von hier?
  go away! gehen Sie weg!
awful furchtbar
axe die Axt
axle die Achse

baby das Baby
back *(not front)* die Rückseite
  (body) der Rücken
  to come back zurückkommen
bacon der Speck
  bacon and eggs Eier mit Speck
bad schlecht
bag die Tasche
baggage claim die Gepäckausgabe
bait der Köder
bake backen
baker der Bäcker
balcony der Balkon
ball der Ball
Baltic die Ostsee
banana die Banane
band *(musicians)* die Band
bandage der Verband
bank die Bank
banknote der (Geld)schein
bar *(drinks)* die Bar
  bar of chocolate die Tafel

Schokolade
barber's der Friseur
bargain das Sonderangebot
basement das Untergeschoß
basin *(sink)* das Becken
basket der Korb
bath das Bad
  (tub) die Badewanne
  to have a bath ein Bad nehmen
bathroom das Badezimmer
battery die Batterie
Bavaria Bayern
beach der Strand
beans die Bohnen
beard der Bart
beautiful schön
because weil
bed das Bett
bed linen die Bettwäsche
bedroom das Schlafzimmer
beef das Rindfleisch
beer das Bier
before ... vor ...
beginner der Anfänger
behind ... hinter ...
beige beige
Belgian *(man)* der Belgier
  (woman) die Belgierin
  (adj) belgisch
Belgium Belgien
bell *(church)* die Glocke
  (door) die Klingel
below ... unter ...
belt der Gürtel
beside neben
best bester
better besser
between ... zwischen ...
bicycle das Fahrrad
big groß
bikini der Bikini
bill die Rechnung
bin liner die Mülltüte
bird der Vogel

Biro ® der Kugelschreiber
birthday der Geburtstag
  happy birthday! viel Glück zum
  Geburtstag!
birthday card die Geburtstagskarte
birthday present das
  Geburtstagsgeschenk
biscuit das Plätzchen
bite *(noun: by dog)* der Biß
  (by insect) der Stich
  (verb) beißen
  (insect) stechen
bitter bitter
black schwarz
blackberry die Brombeere
blackcurrant die schwarze
  Johannisbeere
Black Forest der Schwarzwald
blanket die Decke
bleach *(noun)* das Reinigungsmittel
  (verb: hair) bleichen
blind *(cannot see)* blind
blinds die Jalousie
blister die Blase
blizzard der Schneesturm
blond(e) *(adj)* blond
blonde *(noun)* die Blondine
blood das Blut
blouse die Bluse
blue blau
boat das Schiff
  (small) das Boot
body der Körper
  (corpse) die Leiche
boil *(verb)* kochen
boiler der Boiler
bolt *(noun: on door)* der Riegel
  (verb) verriegeln
bone der Knochen
bonnet *(car)* die Motorhaube
book *(noun)* das Buch
  (verb) buchen
bookshop die Buchhandlung
boot *(car)* der Kofferraum

(footwear) der Stiefel
border die Grenze
boring langweilig
born: I was born in ... ich bin in
  ... geboren
both beide
  both of us wir beide
  both ... and ... sowohl ... als
  auch ...
bottle die Flasche
bottle-opener der Flaschenöffner
bottom der Boden
  (part of body) der Hintern
  (sea) der Grund
bowl die Schüssel
box die Schachtel
box office die Kasse
boy der Junge
boyfriend der Freund
bra der Büstenhalter
bracelet das Armband
braces die Hosenträger
brake *(noun)* die Bremse
  (verb) bremsen
brandy der Weinbrand
bread das Brot
breakdown *(car)* die Panne
  (nervous) der Zusammenbruch
  I've had a breakdown ich habe
  eine Panne
breakfast das Frühstück
breathe atmen
bridge die Brücke
  (game) Bridge
briefcase die Aktentasche
Britain Großbritannien
British britisch
brochure die Broschüre
broken *(leg etc)* gebrochen
  (vase etc) zerbrochen
  (machine etc) kaputt
  broken leg der Beinbruch
brooch die Brosche
brother der Bruder

brown braun
bruise der blaue Fleck
brush *(noun)* die Bürste
  (paint) der Pinsel
  (verb: hair) bürsten
  (floor) kehren
Brussels Brüssel
bucket der Eimer
building das Gebäude
bumper die Stoßstange
burglar der Einbrecher
burn *(noun)* die Verbrennung
  (verb) brennen
bus der Bus
business das Geschäft
  it's none of your business das
  geht Sie nichts an
bus station der Busbahnhof
busy *(occupied)* beschäftigt
  (bar etc) voll
but aber
butcher's die Metzgerei
butter die Butter
button der Knopf
buy kaufen
by: by the window am Fenster
  by Friday bis Freitag
  by myself/himself allein

cabbage der Kohl
cable car die Drahtseilbahn
café das Café
cagoule die Regenhaut ®
cake der Kuchen
cake shop die Konditorei
calculator der Rechner
call: what's it called? wie heißt
  das?
camcorder der Camcorder
camera die Kamera
campsite der Campingplatz
camshaft die Nockenwelle
can *(tin)* die Dose
  can I have ...? kann ich ...

haben?
  can you ...? können Sie ...?
Canada Kanada
Canadian *(man)* der Kanadier
  (woman) die Kanadierin
  (adj) kanadisch
canal der Kanal
candle die Kerze
canoe das Kanu
cap *(bottle)* der Verschluß
  (hat) die Mütze
car das Auto
caravan der Wohnwagen
carburettor der Vergaser
card die Karte
cardigan die Strickjacke
careful sorgfältig
  be careful! passen Sie auf!
caretaker der Hausmeister
carpet der Teppich
carriage *(train)* der Wagen
carrot die Möhre, die Karotte
carry-cot die Säuglingstragetasche
case *(suitcase)* der Koffer
cash *(noun)* das Bargeld
  (verb) einlösen
  to pay cash bar bezahlen
cash dispenser der Geldautomat
cassette die Kassette
cassette player der Kassetten-
recorder
castle das Schloß, die Burg
cat die Katze
cathedral der Dom
cauliflower der Blumenkohl
cave die Höhle
cemetery der Friedhof
central heating die Zentralheizung
centre *(middle)* die Mitte
certificate die Bescheinigung
chair der Stuhl
change *(noun: money)* das Kleingeld
  (verb: money) wechseln
  (clothes) sich umziehen

Channel der Kanal
Channel Tunnel der Kanaltunnel
cheap billig
check-in *(desk)* die Abfertigung
check in *(verb)* einchecken
cheers! prost!
cheese der Käse
chemist's die Apotheke
cheque der Scheck
cheque book das Scheckheft
cheque card die Scheckkarte
cherry die Kirsche
chess Schach
chest *(part of body)* die Brust
    (furniture) die Truhe
chest of drawers die Kommode
chewing gum der Kaugummi
chicken das Huhn
    (cooked) das Hähnchen
child das Kind
children die Kinder
china das Porzellan
chips die Pommes frites
chocolate die Schokolade
    box of chocolates die Schachtel
    Pralinen
chop *(food)* das Kotelett
    (verb: to cut) kleinschneiden
Christian name der Vorname
church die Kirche
cigar die Zigarre
    (thin) das Zigarillo
cigarette die Zigarette
cinema das Kino
city die (Groß)stadt
city centre das Stadtzentrum
class die Klasse
classical music die klassische
    Musik
clean *(adj)* sauber
clear klar
clever klug
cling film die Folie
clock die Uhr

close *(near)* nah
    (stuffy) stickig
    (verb) schließen
closed geschlossen
clothes die Kleider
clubs *(cards)* Kreuz
clutch die Kupplung
coach der Bus
    (train) der Wagen
coach station der Busbahnhof
coat der Mantel
coathanger der (Kleider)bügel
cockroach die Küchenschabe
coffee der Kaffee
coin die Münze
cold *(illness)* die Erkältung
    (adj) kalt
    I have a cold ich bin erkältet
    I am cold mir ist kalt
collar der Kragen
collection *(stamps etc)* die
    Sammlung
    (postal) die Leerung
Cologne Köln
colour die Farbe
colour film der Farbfilm
comb *(noun)* der Kamm
come kommen
    I come from ... ich komme
    aus ...
    we came last week wir sind letzte
    Woche angekommen
    come here! kommen Sie her!
Common Market der gemeinsame
    Markt
compact disc die Compact-Disc
compartment das Abteil
complicated kompliziert
computer der Computer
concert das Konzert
conditioner *(hair)* der Festiger
condom das Kondom
conductor *(bus)* der Schaffner
    (orchestra) der Dirigent

congratulations! herzlichen Glückwunsch!
consulate das Konsulat
contact lenses die Kontaktlinsen
contraceptive das Verhütungsmittel
cook *(noun)* der Koch
  (verb) kochen
cooker der Herd
cooking utensils das Kochgeschirr
cool kühl
cork der Korken
corkscrew der Korkenzieher
corner die Ecke
corridor der Korridor
cosmetics die Kosmetika
cost *(verb)* kosten
  what does it cost? was kostet das?
cotton die Baumwolle
cotton wool die Watte
cough *(noun)* der Husten
  (verb) husten
country das Land
cousin *(male)* der Vetter
  (female) die Kusine
crab die Krabbe
cramp der Krampf
crayfish der Krebs
cream *(for cake etc)* die Sahne
  (lotion) die Creme
credit card die Kreditkarte
crisps die Chips
crowded überfüllt
cruise die Kreuzfahrt
crutches die Krücken
cry *(weep)* weinen
  (shout) rufen
cucumber die Gurke
cufflinks die Manschettenknöpfe
cup die Tasse
cupboard der Schrank
curlers die Lockenwickler

curling tongs der Lockenstab
curls die Locken
curry das Curry
curtain der Vorhang
Customs der Zoll
cut *(noun)* der Schnitt
  (verb) schneiden
Czechoslovakia die Tschechoslowakei

dad der Vater
damp feucht
dance *(noun)* der Tanz
  (verb) tanzen
Dane *(man)* der Däne
  (woman) die Dänin
Danish dänisch
dangerous gefährlich
Danube die Donau
dark dunkel
daughter die Tochter
day der Tag
dead tot
deaf taub
dear *(person)* lieb
  (expensive) teuer
deckchair der Liegestuhl
deep tief
delayed verspätet
deliberately absichtlich
Denmark Dänemark
dentist der Zahnarzt
dentures die Prothese
deny bestreiten
deodorant das Deodorant
department store das Kaufhaus
departure die Abfahrt
departure lounge die Abflughalle
develop *(film)* entwickeln
diamond *(jewel)* der Diamant
diamonds *(cards)* Karo
diarrhoea der Durchfall
diary das Tagebuch
dictionary das Wörterbuch

die sterben
diesel der Diesel
different verschieden
  that's different! das ist etwas
  anderes!
  I'd like a different kind ich
  möchte gern eine andere Sorte
difficult schwierig
dining room der Speiseraum
directory *(telephone)* das
  Telefonbuch
dirty schmutzig
disabled behindert
disposable nappies die
  Papierwindeln
distributor *(car)* der Verteiler
dive *(noun)* der Sprung
  (verb) tauchen
diving board das Sprungbett
divorced geschieden
do tun
  how do you do? guten Tag
  (on being introduced) freut mich
doctor der Arzt
document das Dokument
dog der Hund
doll die Puppe
dollar der Dollar
door die Tür
double room das Doppelzimmer
doughnut der Berliner
down herunter
  (position) unten
  down here hier unten
drawing pin die Heftzwecke
dress das Kleid
drink *(noun)* das Getränk
  (verb) trinken
  would you like a drink?
  möchten Sie etwas trinken?
drinking water das Trinkwasser
drive *(verb)* fahren
driver der Fahrer
driving licence der Führerschein

drunk betrunken
dry trocken
dry-cleaner's die chemische
  Reinigung
dummy *(for baby)* der Schnuller
during während
dustbin die Mülltonne
duster das Staubtuch
Dutch *(adj)* holländisch
Dutchman der Holländer
Dutchwoman die Holländerin
duty-free zollfrei
duvet das Federbett

each *(every)* jeder
  five marks each fünf Mark das
  Stück
ear das Ohr
early früh
earrings die Ohrringe
ears die Ohren
east der Osten
easy leicht
eat essen
EC die EG
egg das Ei
either: either of them einer von
  beiden
  either ... or ... entweder ...
  oder ...
elastic elastisch
elastic band das Gummiband
elbow der Ellbogen
electric elektrisch
electricity der Strom
else: something else etwas anderes
  someone else jemand anders
  somewhere else woanders
embarrassing peinlich
embassy die Botschaft
embroidery die Stickerei
emerald der Smaragd
emergency der Notfall
emergency brake die Notbremse

emergency exit der Notausgang
empty leer
end das Ende
engaged *(couple)* verlobt
 (occupied) besetzt
engine *(motor)* der Motor
England England
English *(adj)* englisch
 (language) Englisch
Englishman der Engländer
Englishwoman die Engländerin
enlargement die Vergrößerung
enough genug
entertainment die Unterhaltung
entrance der Eingang
envelope der (Brief)umschlag
escalator die Rolltreppe
especially besonders
evening der Abend
every jeder
everyone jeder
everything alles
everywhere überall
example das Beispiel
 for example zum Beispiel
excellent ausgezeichnet
excess baggage das Mehrgepäck
exchange *(verb)* (um)tauschen
exchange rate der Wechselkurs
excursion der Ausflug
excuse me! Entschuldigung!
exit der Ausgang
expensive teuer
extension lead die
 Verlängerungsschnur
eye das Auge
 eyes die Augen

face das Gesicht
faint *(unclear)* blaß
 (verb) ohnmächtig werden
fair *(funfair)* der Jahrmarkt
 (just) gerecht, fair
false teeth die Prothese

family die Familie
fan *(ventilator)* der Ventilator
 (enthusiast) der Fan
fan belt der Keilriemen
fantastic fantastisch
far weit
 how far is it? wie weit ist es?
fare der Fahrpreis
farm der Bauernhof
farmer der Bauer
fashion die Mode
fast schnell
fat *(person)* dick
 (on meat etc) das Fett
father der Vater
fax *(noun)* das Fax
 (verb: document) faxen
feel *(touch)* fühlen
 I feel hot mir ist heiß
 I feel like ... ich möchte gern ...
 I don't feel well mir ist nicht gut
feet die Füße
felt-tip pen der Filzstift
fence der Zaun
ferry die Fähre
fever das Fieber
fiancé der Verlobte
fiancée die Verlobte
field das Feld
fig die Feige
filling *(in tooth, cake)* die Füllung
 (in sandwich) der Belag
film der Film
filter der Filter
filter papers das Filterpapier
finger der Finger
fire das Feuer
fire extinguisher der Feuerlöscher
fireworks das Feuerwerk
first erster
 first aid die Erste Hilfe
 first floor der erste Stock
fish der Fisch
fishing das Angeln

to go fishing Angeln gehen
fishmonger's das Fischgeschäft
fizzy sprudelnd
flag die Fahne
flash *(camera)* der Blitz
flat *(level)* flach
  (apartment) die Wohnung
flavour der Geschmack
flea der Floh
flight der Flug
flippers die (Schwimm)flossen
floor *(ground)* der Boden
  (storey) der Stock
flour das Mehl
flower die Blume
flute die Flöte
fly *(insect)* die Fliege
  (verb) fliegen
fog der Nebel
folk music die Volksmusik
food das Essen
food poisoning die
  Lebensmittelvergiftung
foot der Fuß
football der Fußball
for für
  for me für mich
  what for? wofür?
  for a week für eine Woche
foreigner der Ausländer
  (female) die Ausländerin
forest der Wald
forget vergessen
fork die Gabel
fortnight zwei Wochen
fountain pen der Füller
fourth vierter
France Frankreich
free frei
  (no charge) kostenlos
freezer der Gefrierschrank
French französisch
Frenchman der Franzose
Frenchwoman die Französin

fridge der Kühlschrank
friend der Freund
  (female) die Freundin
friendly freundlich
fringe *(hair)* der Pony
front: in front of ... vor ...
frost der Frost
fruit die Frucht
fruit juice der Fruchtsaft
fry braten
frying pan die (Brat)pfanne
full voll
  I'm full (up) ich bin satt
full board Vollpension
funny komisch
furniture die Möbel

garage die Garage
  (for repairs) die Werkstatt
garden der Garten
garlic der Knoblauch
gas-permeable lenses
  luftdurchlässige Kontaktlinsen
gate das Tor
  (at airport) der Flugsteig
gay *(homosexual)* schwul
gear der Gang
gear lever der Schaltknüppel
gel *(hair)* das Gel
gents *(toilet)* die Herrentoilette
German *(man)* der Deutsche
  (woman) die Deutsche
  (adj) deutsch
  (language) Deutsch
Germany Deutschland
get *(fetch)* holen
  have you got ...? haben Sie ...?
  to get the train den Zug nehmen
get back: we get back tomorrow
  wir kommen morgen zurück
  to get something back etwas
  zurückbekommen
get in hereinkommen
  (arrive) ankommen

get off *(bus etc)* aussteigen
get on *(bus etc)* einsteigen
get out herauskommen
   (bring out) herausholen
get up *(rise)* aufstehen
gift das Geschenk
gin der Gin
ginger *(spice)* der Ingwer
girl das Mädchen
girlfriend die Freundin
give geben
glad froh
glass das Glas
glasses die Brille
gloss prints die Glanzabzüge
gloves die Handschuhe
glue der Leim
go gehen
   (travel) fahren
   (by plane) fliegen
gold das Gold
good gut
goodbye auf Wiedersehen
government die Regierung
granddaughter die Enkelin
grandfather der Großvater
grandmother die Großmutter
grandparents die Großeltern
grandson der Enkel
grapes die Trauben
grass das Gras
great: great! prima!
Great Britain Großbritannien
green grün
grey grau
grill der Grill
grocer's das Lebensmittelgeschäft
ground floor das Erdgeschoß
groundsheet die Bodenplane
guarantee *(noun)* die Garantie
   (verb) garantieren
guard der Wächter
guide der Führer
guide book der (Reise)führer

guitar die Gitarre
gun *(rifle)* das Gewehr
   (pistol) die Pistole

hair das Haar
haircut der Haarschnitt
hairdresser's der Friseur
hair dryer der Haartrockner
hair spray das Haarspray
half halb
   half an hour eine halbe Stunde
half board Halbpension
ham der Schinken
hamburger der Hamburger
hammer der Hammer
hand die Hand
handbag die Handtasche
handbrake die Handbremse
handkerchief das Taschentuch
handle *(door)* die Klinke
handsome gutaussehend
hangover der Kater
happy glücklich
harbour der Hafen
hard hart
   (difficult) schwer
hard lenses harte Kontaktlinsen
hat der Hut
have haben
   I have ... ich habe ...
   have you got ...? haben Sie ...?
   I have to go ich muß gehen
hayfever der Heuschnupfen
he er
head der Kopf
headache die Kopfschmerzen
headlights die Scheinwerfer
hear hören
hearing aid das Hörgerät
heart das Herz
hearts *(cards)* Herz
heater das Heizgerät
heating die Heizung
heavy schwer

heel *(shoe)* der Absatz
(foot) die Ferse
hello guten Tag
(on phone) hallo
help *(noun)* die Hilfe
(verb) helfen
her: it's her sie ist es
it's for her es ist für sie
give it to her geben Sie es ihr
her book ihr Buch
her shoes ihre Schuhe
it's hers es gehört ihr
hi hallo
high hoch
highway code die
Straßenverkehrsordnung
hill der Berg
him: it's him er ist es
it's for him es ist für ihn
give it to him geben Sie es ihm
hire leihen
his: his book sein Buch
his shoes seine Schuhe
it's his es gehört ihm
history die Geschichte
hitch-hike trampen
hobby das Hobby
Holland Holland
holiday der Urlaub
home: at home zu Hause
honest ehrlich
honey der Honig
honeymoon die Hochzeitsreise
horn *(car)* die Hupe
(animal) das Horn
horrible schrecklich
hospital das Krankenhaus
hour die Stunde
house das Haus
how? wie?
hungry: I'm hungry ich habe
Hunger
hurry: I'm in a hurry ich bin in
Eile

husband der (Ehe)mann

I ich
ice das Eis
ice cream das Eis, die Eiscreme
ice lolly das Eis am Stiel
ice skates die Schlittschuhe
ice skating: to go ice skating
Schlittschuhlaufen gehen
if wenn
ignition die Zündung
ill krank
immediately sofort
impossible unmöglich
in in
in English auf Englisch
in the hotel im Hotel
indicator der Blinker
indigestion die
Magenverstimmung
infection die Infektion
information die Information
injection die Spritze
injury die Verletzung
ink die Tinte
inn das Gasthaus
inner tube der Schlauch
insect das Insekt
insect repellent das Insektenmittel
insomnia die Schlaflosigkeit
instant coffee der Pulverkaffee
insurance die Versicherung
interesting interessant
interpret dolmetschen
interpreter der Dolmetscher
(female) die Dolmetscherin
invitation die Einladung
Ireland Irland
Irish irisch
Irishman der Ire
Irishwoman die Irin
iron *(material)* das Eisen
(for clothes) das Bügeleisen
(verb) bügeln

is: he/she/it is ... er/sie/es ist ...
island die Insel
it es
Italian *(man)* der Italiener
  (woman) die Italienerin
  (adj) italienisch
Italy Italien
itch *(noun)* das Jucken

jacket die Jacke
jam die Marmelade
jazz der Jazz
jeans die Jeans
jellyfish die Qualle
jeweller's das Juweliergeschäft
jewellery der Schmuck
job die Arbeit
jog *(verb)* joggen
  to go for a jog joggen gehen
joke der Witz
journey die Reise
jumper der Pullover
just *(only)* nur
  it's just arrived es ist gerade
  angekommen

kettle der Wasserkessel
key der Schlüssel
kidney die Niere
kilo das Kilo
kilometre der Kilometer
kitchen die Küche
knee das Knie
knife das Messer
knit stricken
knitwear die Strickwaren
know wissen
  (be acquainted with) kennen
  I don't know ich weiß nicht

label das Etikett
lace die Spitze
laces *(shoe)* die Schnürsenkel
ladies *(toilet)* die Damentoilette

lady die Dame
lake der See
Lake Constance der Bodensee
lamb *(animal)* das Lamm
  (meat) das Lammfleisch
lamp die Lampe
lampshade der Lampenschirm
land *(noun)* das Land
  (verb) landen
language die Sprache
large groß
last *(final)* letzter
  last week letzte Woche
  at last! endlich!
late spät
  the bus is late der Bus hat
  Verspätung
later später
laugh lachen
launderette der Waschsalon
laundry *(place)* die Wäscherei
  (dirty clothes) die Wäsche
laxative das Abführmittel
lazy faul
leadfree bleifrei
leaf das Blatt
leaflet die Broschüre
learn lernen
leather das Leder
left *(not right)* links
  there's nothing left es ist nichts
  mehr übrig
left luggage locker das Gepäck-
  schließfach
leg das Bein
lemon die Zitrone
lemonade die Limonade
length die Länge
lens die Linse
less weniger
lesson die Stunde
letter *(post)* der Brief
  (alphabet) der Buchstabe
letter box der Briefkasten

lettuce der Kopfsalat
library die Bücherei
licence die Genehmigung
life das Leben
lift *(in building)* der Fahrstuhl
  could you give me a lift? können
  Sie mich mitnehmen?
light *(noun)* das Licht
  (adj: not heavy) leicht
  (not dark) hell
light bulb die (Glüh)birne
light meter der Belichtungsmesser
lighter das Feuerzeug
lighter fuel das Feuerzeugbenzin
like: I like you ich mag Sie
  I like swimming ich schwimme
  gern
  it's like ... es ist wie ...
  like this so
lime *(fruit)* die Limone
lip salve der Lippen-Fettstift
lipstick der Lippenstift
liqueur der Likör
list die Liste
litre der Liter
litter der Abfall
little *(small)* klein
  it's a little big es ist ein bißchen
  zu groß
  just a little nur ein bißchen
liver die Leber
lobster der Hummer
lollipop der Lutscher
long lang
lorry der Lastwagen
lost property das Fundbüro
lot: a lot viel
loud laut
  (colour) grell
lounge das Wohnzimmer
  (in hotel) die Lounge
love *(noun)* die Liebe
  (verb) lieben
lover *(man)* der Liebhaber

  (woman) die Geliebte
low niedrig
  (voice) tief
luck das Glück
  good luck! viel Glück!
luggage das Gepäck
luggage rack die Gepäckablage
lunch das Mittagessen
Luxembourg Luxemburg

mad verrückt
magazine die Zeitschrift
mail die Post
make machen
make-up das Make-up
man der Mann
manager der Geschäftsführer
many: not many nicht viele
map *(of country)* die Landkarte
  (of town) der Stadtplan
marble der Marmor
margarine die Margarine
market der Markt
marmalade die
  Orangenmarmelade
married verheiratet
mascara die Wimperntusche
mass *(church)* die Messe
match *(light)* das Streichholz
  (sport) das Spiel
material *(cloth)* der Stoff
matter: it doesn't matter das
  macht nichts
mattress die Matratze
maybe vielleicht
me: it's me ich bin's
  it's for me es ist für mich
  give it to me geben Sie es mir
meal das Essen
mean: what does this mean? was
  bedeutet das?
meat das Fleisch
mechanic der Mechaniker
medicine die Medizin

meeting das Treffen
melon die Melone
menu die Speisekarte
message die Nachricht
midday der Mittag
middle: in the middle in der Mitte
midnight Mitternacht
milk die Milch
mine: it's mine es gehört mir
mineral water das Mineralwasser
minute die Minute
mirror der Spiegel
Miss Fräulein
mistake der Fehler
money das Geld
month der Monat
monument das Denkmal
moon der Mond
moped das Moped
more mehr
morning der Morgen
  in the morning am Morgen
mother die Mutter
motorbike das Motorrad
motorboat das Motorboot
motorway die Autobahn
mountain der Berg
mountain bike das Mountain-Bike
mouse die Maus
mousse *(for hair)* der Schaum-
  festiger
moustache der Schnurrbart
mouth der Mund
move *(verb)* bewegen
  (house) umziehen
  don't move! stillhalten!
movie der Film
Mr Herr
Mrs Frau
Ms Frau
much viel
mum die Mutter
Munich München
museum das Museum

mushroom der Pilz
music die Musik
musical instrument das
  Musikinstrument
musician der Musiker
mussels die Muscheln
must: I must ... ich muß ...
mustard der Senf
my: my book mein Buch
  my keys meine Schlüssel

nail *(metal, finger)* der Nagel
nail clippers der Nagelzwicker
nail file die Nagelfeile
nail polish der Nagellack
name der Name
  what's your name? wie heißen
  Sie?
nappy die Windel
narrow eng
near nah
  near the door nahe der Tür
  near London in der Nähe von
  London
necessary nötig
neck der Hals
necklace die Halskette
need *(verb)* brauchen
  I need ... ich brauche ...
  there's no need das ist nicht
  nötig
needle die Nadel
negative *(photo)* das Negativ
neither: neither of them keiner
  von ihnen
  neither ... nor ... weder ...
  noch ...
nephew der Neffe
Netherlands die Niederlande
never nie
new neu
news die Nachrichten
newsagent's der Zeitungsladen
newspaper die Zeitung

New Zealand Neuseeland
New Zealander *(man)* der
  Neuseeländer
  (woman) die Neuseeländerin
next nächster
  next week nächste Woche
nice *(attractive)* hübsch
  (pleasant) angenehm
  (to eat) lecker
niece die Nichte
night die Nacht
nightclub der Nachtklub
nightdress das Nachthemd
night porter der Nachtportier
no *(response)* nein
  I have no money ich habe kein
  Geld
noisy laut
north der Norden
Northern Ireland Nordirland
North Sea die Nordsee
nose die Nase
not nicht
notebook das Notizbuch
nothing nichts
novel der Roman
now jetzt
nowhere nirgendwo
nudist der Nudist
number die Zahl
  (telephone) die Nummer
number plate das Nummernschild
nursery slope der Idiotenhügel
nut *(fruit)* die Nuß
  (for bolt) die Mutter

occasionally gelegentlich
of von
  the name of the hotel der Name
  des Hotels
office das Büro
often oft
oil das Öl
ointment die Salbe

OK okay
old alt
  how old are you? wie alt sind
  Sie?
olive die Olive
omelette das Omelette
on ... auf ...
one *(number)* eins
  one beer/sausage ein Bier/eine
  Wurst
onion die Zwiebel
only nur
open *(verb)* öffnen
  (adj) offen
operation die Operation
operator die Vermittlung
opposite: opposite the hotel
  gegenüber dem Hotel
optician der Augenarzt
or oder
orange *(colour)* orange
  (fruit) die Orange
orange juice der Orangensaft
orchestra das Orchester
ordinary gewöhnlich
other: the other ... der/die/das
  andere ...
our unser
  it's ours es gehört uns
out aus
  he's out er ist nicht da
outside außerhalb
oven der Backofen
over *(more than)* über
  (finished) vorbei
  (across) über
  over there dort drüben
overtake überholen
oyster die Auster

pack of cards das Kartenspiel
package *(parcel)* das Paket
packet das Paket
  (of cigarettes) die Schachtel

padlock das Vorhängeschloß
page die Seite
pain der Schmerz
paint *(noun)* die Farbe
pair das Paar
palace der Palast
pale blaß
pancake der Pfannkuchen
paper das Papier
(newspaper) die Zeitung
paracetamol die Schmerztablette
paraffin das Paraffin
parcel das Paket
pardon? bitte?
parents die Eltern
park *(noun)* der Park
(verb) parken
parsley die Petersilie
parting *(hair)* der Scheitel
party *(celebration)* die Party
(group) die Gruppe
(political) die Partei
passenger der Passagier
passport der Paß
pasta die Nudeln
path der Weg
pavement der Bürgersteig
pay bezahlen
peach der Pfirsich
peanuts die Erdnüsse
pear die Birne
pearl die Perle
peas die Erbsen
pedestrian der Fußgänger
peg *(clothes)* die Wäscheklammer
(tent) der Hering
pen der Stift
pencil der Bleistift
pencil sharpener der
Bleistiftspitzer
penfriend der Brieffreund
(female) die Brieffreundin
penknife das Taschenmesser
people die Leute

pepper der Pfeffer
(red/green) der Paprika
peppermints die
Pfefferminzbonbons
per: per night pro Nacht
perfect perfekt
perfume das Parfüm
perhaps vielleicht
perm die Dauerwelle
petrol das Benzin
petrol station die Tankstelle
photograph *(noun)* das Foto
(verb) fotografieren
photographer der Fotograf
phrase book der Sprachführer
piano das Klavier
pickpocket der Taschendieb
picnic das Picknick
piece das Stück
pillow das Kopfkissen
pilot der Pilot
pin die Stecknadel
pineapple die Ananas
pink rosa
pipe *(for smoking)* die Pfeife
(for water) das Rohr
piston der Kolben
pizza die Pizza
place der Platz
(town etc) der Ort
at your place bei Ihnen
plant die Pflanze
plaster *(for cut)* das Pflaster
plastic das Plastik
plastic bag die Plastiktüte
plate der Teller
platform der Bahnsteig
play *(theatre)* das Stück
(verb) spielen
please bitte
plug *(electrical)* der Stecker
(sink) der Stöpsel
pocket die Tasche
poison das Gift

Poland Polen
Pole *(man)* der Pole
   (woman) die Polin
Polish polnisch
police die Polizei
policeman der Polizist
police station das Polizeirevier
politics die Politik
poor arm
   (bad quality) schlecht
pop music die Popmusik
pork das Schweinefleisch
port *(harbour)* der Hafen
   (drink) der Portwein
porter *(hotel)* der Portier
possible möglich
post *(noun)* die Post
   (verb) aufgeben
post box der Briefkasten
postcard die Postkarte
poster das Poster
postman der Briefträger
post office das Postamt
potato die Kartoffel
poultry das Geflügel
pound *(money, weight)* das Pfund
powder das Pulver
   (cosmetics) der Puder
pram der Kinderwagen
prawns die Krabben
prefer: I prefer ... ich mag
   lieber ...
prescription das Rezept
pretty *(beautiful)* schön
   (quite) ziemlich
pretty good recht gut
priest der Geistliche
private privat
problem das Problem
public öffentlich
pull ziehen
puncture die Reifenpanne
purple lila
purse das Portemonnaie

push drücken
pushchair der Sportwagen
put tun
pyjamas der Schlafanzug

quality die Qualität
quarter das Viertel
quay der Kai
question die Frage
queue *(noun)* die Schlange
   (verb) anstehen
quick schnell
quiet ruhig
quite *(fairly)* ziemlich
   (fully) ganz

radiator der Heizkörper
   (car) der Kühler
radio das Radio
radish der Rettich
   (small red) das Radieschen
railway die Bahn
rain der Regen
raincoat der Regenmantel
raisins die Rosinen
rare *(uncommon)* selten
   (steak) englisch
raspberries die Himbeeren
rat die Ratte
razor blades die Rasierklingen
read lesen
reading lamp die Leselampe
ready fertig
rear lights die Rücklichter
receipt die Quittung
receptionist die Empfangsperson
record *(music)* die Schallplatte
   (sporting etc) der Rekord
record player der Plattenspieler
record shop das Schallplatten-
   geschäft
red rot
refreshments die Erfrischungen
relative der Verwandte

relax sich entspannen

religion die Religion

remember sich erinnern
  I don't remember ich erinnere
  mich nicht

rent *(verb)* mieten

reservation die Reservierung

rest *(noun: remainder)* der Rest
  (verb: relax) sich ausruhen

restaurant das Restaurant

restaurant car der Speisewagen

return *(come back)* zurückkommen
  (give back) zurückgeben

return ticket die Rückfahrkarte

rice der Reis

rich reich

right *(correct)* richtig
  (direction) rechts

ring *(to call)* anrufen
  (wedding etc) der Ring

ripe reif

river der Fluß

road die Straße

rock *(stone)* der Stein
  (music) der Rock

roll *(bread)* das Brötchen

roof das Dach

room das Zimmer
  (space) der Raum

rope das Seil

rose die Rose

round *(circular)* rund
  it's my round das ist meine
  Runde

rowing boat das Ruderboot

rubber *(eraser)* der Radiergummi
  (material) das Gummi

rubbish der Abfall

ruby *(stone)* der Rubin

rucksack der Rucksack

rug *(mat)* der Läufer
  (blanket) die Wolldecke

ruins die Ruinen

ruler *(for drawing)* das Lineal

rum der Rum

run *(verb)* laufen

runway die Start- und Landebahn

sad traurig

safe sicher

safety pin die Sicherheitsnadel

sailing boat das Segelboot

salad der Salat

salami die Salami

sale *(at reduced prices)* der
  Schlußverkauf

salmon der Lachs

salt das Salz

same: the same dress das gleiche
  Kleid
  same again please nochmal
  dasselbe, bitte

sand der Sand

sandals die Sandalen

sandwich das Butterbrot

sanitary towels die Damenbinden

sauce die Soße

saucepan der Kochtopf

sauna die Sauna

sausage die Wurst

say sagen
  what did you say? was haben Sie
  gesagt?
  how do you say ...? wie sagt
  man ...?

Scandinavia Skandinavien

scarf der Schal
  (head) das Kopftuch

school die Schule

scissors die Schere

Scotland Schottland

Scotsman der Schotte

Scotswoman die Schottin

Scottish schottisch

screw die Schraube

screwdriver der Schraubenzieher

sea das Meer

seafood die Meeresfrüchte

seat der Sitz
seat belt der Sicherheitsgurt
second *(time)* die Sekunde
(in series) zweiter
see sehen
  I can't see ich kann nichts sehen
  I see ich verstehe
sell verkaufen
sellotape ® der Tesafilm ®
separate getrennt
separately getrennt
separated: we are separated wir
  leben getrennt
serious ernst
serviette die Serviette
several mehrere
sew nähen
shampoo das Shampoo
shave: to have a shave sich
  rasieren
shaving foam die Rasiercreme
shawl das Umhängetuch
she sie
sheet das (Bett)laken
shell die Muschel
shellfish *(to eat)* die Meeresfrüchte
sherry der Sherry
ship das Schiff
shirt das Hemd
shoe laces die Schnürsenkel
shoe polish die Schuhcreme
shoes die Schuhe
shop das Geschäft
shopping das Einkaufen
  (items bought) die Einkäufe
  to go shopping einkaufen gehen
short kurz
shorts die Shorts
shoulder die Schulter
shower *(bath)* die Dusche
  (rain) der Schauer
shrimps die Garnelen
shutter *(camera)* der Verschluß
  (window) der Fensterladen

sick *(ill)* krank
  I feel sick mir ist übel
  to be sick *(vomit)* sich übergeben
side die Seite
  (edge) die Kante
sidelights das Standlicht
sights: the sights of ... die
  Sehenswürdigkeiten von ...
silk die Seide
silver *(colour)* silber
  (metal) das Silber
simple einfach
sing singen
single *(one)* einziger
  (unmarried) ledig
single room das Einzelzimmer
sister die Schwester
ski *(verb)* Ski fahren
ski binding die Skibindung
ski boots die Skistiefel
skid *(verb)* schleudern
skiing: to go skiing Skifahren
  gehen
ski lift der Skilift
skin cleanser der Hautreiniger
ski resort der Skiurlaubsort
skirt der Rock
skis die Skier
ski sticks die Skistöcke
sky der Himmel
sledge der Schlitten
sleep *(noun)* der Schlaf
  (verb) schlafen
sleeping bag der Schlafsack
sleeping pill die Schlaftablette
slippers die Pantoffeln
slow langsam
small klein
smell *(noun)* der Geruch
  (verb) riechen
smile *(noun)* das Lächeln
  (verb) lächeln
smoke *(noun)* der Rauch
  (verb) rauchen

snack der Imbiß
snow der Schnee
so so
  not so much nicht so viel
soaking solution *(for contact lenses)* die Aufbewahrungslösung
soap die Seife
socks die Strümpfe
soda water das Sodawasser
soft lenses weiche Kontaktlinsen
somebody jemand
somehow irgendwie
something etwas
sometimes manchmal
somewhere irgendwo
son der Sohn
song das Lied
sorry! *(apology)* Verzeihung!
  I'm sorry es tut mir leid
  sorry? *(pardon)* bitte?
soup die Suppe
south der Süden
South Africa Südafrika
souvenir das Souvenir
spa der Kurort
spade *(shovel)* der Spaten
spades *(cards)* Pik
spanner der Schraubenschlüssel
spares die Ersatzteile
spark(ing) plug die Zündkerze
speak sprechen
  do you speak English? sprechen Sie Englisch?
  I don't speak German ich spreche kein Deutsch
speed die Geschwindigkeit
spider die Spinne
spinach der Spinat
spoon der Löffel
sports centre das Sportzentrum
spring *(mechanical)* die Feder
  (season) der Frühling
square *(shape)* das Quadrat
  (in town) der Platz

stadium das Stadion
staircase die Treppe
stairs die Treppe
stamp die Briefmarke
stapler der Hefter
star der Stern
  (film) der Star
start der Start, der Anfang
  (verb) anfangen
station der Bahnhof
  (tube) die Station
statue die Statue
steak das Steak
steal stehlen
  it's been stolen es ist gestohlen worden
steamer *(boat)* der Dampfer
  (cooking) der Dampfkochtopf
steering wheel das Lenkrad
sting *(noun)* der Stich
  (verb) stechen
stockings die Strümpfe
stomach der Magen
stomach ache die Magenschmerzen
stop *(bus stop)* die Haltestelle
  (verb) anhalten
  stop! halt!
storm der Sturm
strawberries die Erdbeeren
stream *(small river)* der Bach
street die Straße
string *(cord)* der Faden
  (guitar etc) die Saite
strong *(person, drink)* stark
  (material) stabil
  (taste) streng
student der Student
  (female) die Studentin
stupid dumm
suburbs der Stadtrand
sugar der Zucker
suit *(noun)* der Anzug
  it suits you es steht Ihnen

suitcase der Koffer
sun die Sonne
sunbathe sonnenbaden
sunburn der Sonnenbrand
sunglasses die Sonnenbrille
sunny: it's sunny es ist sonnig
sunshade der Sonnenschirm
suntan: to get a suntan braun
  werden
suntan lotion das Sonnenöl
suntanned braungebrannt
supermarket der Supermarkt
supper das Abendessen
supplement der Zuschlag
sure sicher
surname der Nachname
sweat *(noun)* der Schweiß
  (verb) schwitzen
sweatshirt das Sweatshirt
sweet *(not sour)* süß
  (candy) die Süßigkeit
swim *(verb)* schwimmen
swimming costume das
  Badekostüm
swimming pool das Schwimmbad
swimming trunks die Badehose
Swiss *(man)* der Schweizer
  (woman) die Schweizerin
  (adj) schweizerisch
switch der Schalter
Switzerland die Schweiz
synagogue die Synagoge

table der Tisch
tablet die Tablette
take nehmen
take-away der Schnellimbiß
take-off der Abflug
talcum powder das Körperpuder
talk *(noun)* das Gespräch
  (verb) reden
tall groß
tampons die Tampons
tangerine die Mandarine

tap der Hahn
tapestry der Wandteppich
tea der Tee
teacher der Lehrer
  (female) die Lehrerin
tea towel das Geschirrtuch
telegram das Telegramm
telephone *(noun)* das Telefon
  (verb) telefonieren
telephone box die Telefonzelle
television das Fernsehen
  to watch television fernsehen
temperature die Temperatur
  (fever) das Fieber
tent das Zelt
tent peg der Hering
tent pole die Zeltstange
than: bigger than größer als
thank *(verb)* danken
  thanks danke
  thank you danke schön
that: that man dieser Mann
  that woman diese Frau
  what's that? was ist das?
  I think that … ich denke, daß …
the der, die, das
  (pl) die
their: their room ihr Zimmer
  their books ihre Bücher
  it's theirs es gehört ihnen
them: it's them sie sind es
  it's for them es ist für sie
  give it to them geben Sie es
  ihnen
then dann
there da
  there is/are … es gibt …
  is/are there …? gibt es …?
thermos flask die Thermosflasche
these diese
they sie
thick dick
thin dünn
think denken

I think so ich glaube ja
I'll think about it ich überlege es mir
third dritter
thirsty durstig
  I'm thirsty ich habe Durst
this: this man dieser Mann
  this woman diese Frau
  what's this? was ist das?
  this is Mr ... das ist Herr ...
those diese da
  those things die Dinge dort
throat die Kehle
throat pastilles die Halstabletten
through durch
thunderstorm das Gewitter
ticket die Karte
tide: high tide die Flut
  low tide die Ebbe
tie *(noun)* die Krawatte
  (verb) festmachen
tight eng
tights die Strumpfhose
time die Zeit
  what's the time? wie spät ist es?
timetable *(train, bus)* der Fahrplan
tin die Dose
tin-opener der Dosenöffner
tip *(money)* das Trinkgeld
  (end) die Spitze
tired müde
tissues die Papiertücher
to: to England nach England
  to the station zum Bahnhof
  to the doctor zum Arzt
toast der Toast
tobacco der Tabak
toboggan der Schlitten
today heute
together zusammen
toilet die Toilette
toilet paper das Toilettenpapier
tomato die Tomate
tomato juice der Tomatensaft

tomorrow morgen
tongue die Zunge
tonic das Tonic
tonight heute abend
too *(also)* auch
  (excessively) zu
tooth der Zahn
toothache die Zahnschmerzen
toothbrush die Zahnbürste
toothpaste die Zahnpasta
torch die Taschenlampe
tour die Rundreise
tour guide der Reiseleiter
  (female) die Reiseleiterin
tourist der Tourist
  (female) die Touristin
tourist office das Fremdenverkehrsbüro
towel das Handtuch
tower der Turm
town die Stadt
town hall das Rathaus
toy das Spielzeug
track suit der Trainingsanzug
tractor der Traktor
tradition die Tradition
traffic der Verkehr
traffic jam der Stau
traffic lights die Ampel
trailer der Anhänger
train der Zug
trainers die Turnschuhe
translate übersetzen
translator der Übersetzer
  (female) die Übersetzerin
travel agency das Reisebüro
traveller's cheque der Reisescheck
tray das Tablett
tree der Baum
trousers die Hose
true wahr
try versuchen
tunnel der Tunnel
Turk *(man)* der Türke

(woman) die Türkin
Turkey die Türkei
Turkish türkisch
tweezers die Pinzette
typewriter die Schreibmaschine
tyre der Reifen

umbrella der (Regen)schirm
uncle der Onkel
under ... unter ...
underground die U-Bahn
underpants die Unterhose
underskirt der Unterrock
understand verstehen
  I don't understand ich verstehe
  nicht
underwear die Unterwäsche
university die Universität
unleaded bleifrei
until bis
unusual ungewöhnlich
up oben
  (upwards) nach oben
  up there da oben
urgent dringend
us: it's us wir sind es
  it's for us es ist für uns
  give it to us geben Sie es uns
use *(noun)* der Gebrauch
  (verb) gebrauchen
  it's no use es hat keinen Zweck
useful hilfreich
usual gewöhnlich
usually gewöhnlich

vacancy *(room)* ein freies Zimmer
vacuum cleaner der Staubsauger
valley das Tal
valve das Ventil
vanilla die Vanille
vase die Vase
veal das Kalbfleisch
vegetable das Gemüse
vegetarian der Vegetarier

(female) die Vegetarierin
  (adj) vegetarisch
vehicle das Fahrzeug
very sehr
vest das Unterhemd
video *(tape, film)* das Video
video recorder der Videorecorder
Vienna Wien
view der Blick
viewfinder der Sucher
villa die Villa
village das Dorf
vinegar der Essig
violin die Violine
visit *(noun)* der Besuch
  (verb) besuchen
visitor der Besucher
  (female) die Besucherin
vitamin tablet die Vitamintablette
vodka der Wodka
voice die Stimme

wait warten
  wait! warten Sie!
waiter der Ober
  waiter! Herr Ober!
waiting room das Wartezimmer
  (station) der Wartesaal
waitress die Kellnerin
  waitress! Fräulein!
Wales Wales
walk *(noun: stroll)* der Spaziergang
  (verb) gehen
  to go for a walk spazieren gehen
walkman ® der Walkman ®
wall *(inside)* die Wand
  (outside) die Mauer
wallet die Brieftasche
war der Krieg
wardrobe der Kleiderschrank
warm warm
was: I was ich war
  he/she/it was er/sie/es war
washing powder das Waschpulver

143

washing-up liquid das Spülmittel
wasp die Wespe
watch *(noun)* die (Armband)uhr
  (verb) ansehen
water das Wasser
waterfall der Wasserfall
water heater das Heißwassergerät
wave *(noun)* die Welle
  (verb: with hand) winken
wavy *(hair)* wellig
we wir
weather das Wetter
wedding die Hochzeit
week die Woche
welcome willkommen
  you're welcome keine Ursache
wellingtons die Gummistiefel
Welsh walisisch
Welshman der Waliser
Welshwoman die Waliserin
were: we/they were wir/sie waren
  you were Sie waren
  (sing, familiar) du warst
west der Westen
wet naß
what? was?
wheel das Rad
wheelchair der Rollstuhl
when? wann?
where? wo?
whether ob
which? welcher?
whisky der Whisky
white weiß
who? wer?
why? warum?
wide breit
wife die (Ehe)frau
wind der Wind
window das Fenster
wine der Wein
wing der Flügel
with mit
without ohne

woman die Frau
wood *(material)* das Holz
wool die Wolle
word das Wort
work *(noun)* die Arbeit
  (verb) arbeiten
  (machine etc) funktionieren
worse schlechter
worst schlechtester
wrapping paper das Packpapier
  (for presents) das Geschenkpapier
wrist das Handgelenk
writing paper das Schreibpapier
wrong falsch

year das Jahr
yellow gelb
yes ja
yesterday gestern
yet: is it ready yet? ist es schon
  fertig?
  not yet noch nicht
yoghurt der Joghurt
you Sie
  (sing, familiar) du
  for you für Sie/dich
  with you mit Ihnen/dir
your Ihr
  (sing, familiar) dein
  your shoes Ihre/deine Schuhe
yours: is this yours? gehört das
  Ihnen?
  (familiar) gehört das dir?
youth hostel die Jugendherberge

zip der Reißverschluß
zoo der Zoo